"Marty Machowski's Bible-saturated, gospel-shaped writing has been a blessing to my family. As a pastor, his devotionals are my go-to resource for family worship. Marty has the heart of a shepherd, the wisdom of a sage, and provides hope-filled refreshment to any parent who is weary or discouraged. *Parenting First Aid* is a wonderful book that has my highest endorsement, and I encourage you to pick up a copy today."

Josh Mulvihill, Executive Director of Church and Family Ministry at Renewanation; founder of GospelShapedFamily.com

"Parents can wisely face elephant-sized challenges with youth— but best with only one forkful of wisdom at a time. Machowski's book serves God's wise counsel in bite-size devotionals. This is not so much about *what to do* as a parent as it is about *who to be.* The lessons are brief, interesting, and with practical instruction that you can apply immediately. If challenging parenting drains you, exasperates you, confuses you, frustrates you, these weekly meals will nurture you."

Rick Horne, Author of *Get Outta My Face!: How to Reach Angry, Unmotivated Teens with Biblical Counsel* and *Get Offa My Case!: Godly Parenting of an Angry Teen*

"Many Christian parents have a rich knowledge of God's Word, but they don't always understand how to apply that knowledge to the parenting trials God sends their way and can find themselves in a desert of parenting worries. In *Parenting First Aid*, Machowski brings the refreshment of Scripture to that desert. I found myself in tears as the rivers of the Word flowed into some parched corners of my life."

Chap Bettis, Executive Director of The Apollos Project; author of *The Disciple-Making Parent*

"Parenting is challenging work. It's also a gift from a God and a unique opportunity to display God's glory as we lovingly shepherd our children and teach them the gospel of Christ. Marty Machowski's new book, *Parenting First Aid*, is a timely and encouraging reminder for parents to persevere. Every weary parent needs this book."

R. Albert Mohler, Jr., President of the Southern Baptist Theological Seminary

"If you've got parenting figured out, this book is not for you. For the rest of us, here is good medicine from God's Word— not for our child's heart, but for ours. As I read, I was repeatedly refreshed by Marty's unblinking candor about the challenges of children and the faithfulness of God. In these pages, you'll find wisdom for the weary and hope for the hurting."

Champ Thornton, Pastor; author of *The Radical Book for Kids* and *Pass It On: A Proverbs Journal for the Next Generation*

"God has given my wife and me the privilege of parenting four children, each one adopted as an older child from backgrounds of neglect, trauma, and abuse. What a delightful gift Marty Machowski has provided for parents like us—parents for whom there are days when 'success' is simply surviving and loving one another to the end of the day. *Parenting First Aid* is gentle, honest, raw, and wholly centered on the gospel of Jesus Christ."

Timothy Paul Jones, Author of *Family Ministry Field Guide*; C. Edwin Gheens Chair of Christian Family Ministry, The Southern Baptist Theological Seminary

Parenting First Aid

Parenting First Aid

Hope for the Discouraged

MARTY MACHOWSKI

New Growth Press
WWW.NEWGROWTHPRESS.COM

New Growth Press, Greensboro, NC 27404
www.newgrowthpress.com
Copyright © 2018 by Marty Machowski

Cover Design: Faceout Books, faceoutstudio.com
Interior Typesetting and eBook: Lisa Parnell, lparnell.com

ISBN 978-1-945270-99-4 (Print)
ISBN 978-1-948130-00-4 (eBook)

Library of Congress Cataloging-in-Publication Data

Printed in the United States of America

25 24 23 22 21 20 19 18   1 2 3 4 5

Dedication

I dedicate this book to my wife, Lois,
my partner in parenting
and best friend.

To Lois:
I trust, my love, when you read these pages,
that tears of gratitude for our Lord will fill your eyes
as they have mine.
For only by his grace have we come this far
and only by his grace shall we remain.

Contents

Contents

Acknowledgments

I'd like to thank Barbara Juliani and the New Growth Press team for their enthusiasm for this project, and the many friends who read through the drafts of this book. In particular, the feedback of Sean Taylor, Joel Bain, Nick Kidwell, and Jim Donohue leaves their imprint. I am grateful for the folks who generously allowed me to share their stories within these pages to help encourage your soul. Most of all, I'd like to thank my wife, Lois, and my children, who gave their enthusiastic permission for me to put their lives on display in these pages and were glad to listen as I read each new paragraph.

Introduction

Apart from the first two months of sleepless nights and the time later spent working through potty training, I started out a confident parent. I read every recommended parenting book I could get my hands on and was determined to be a great dad. How difficult could parenting be? I planned to simply drive the foolishness from my children with consistent, loving discipline. I firmly believed the Bible verse that promised that if I simply trained my children up in the way they should go, they would not depart from it. You can read it for yourself in Proverbs 22:6. Being a military man, I believed effective parenting depended on effective discipline.

I remember hearing Tedd Tripp share a message at Westminster Theological Seminary around the time that his groundbreaking book, *Shepherding a Child's Heart*, was released. My wife, Lois, and I were only two years into parenting at that point, and I remember thinking, *This is the piece we're missing*. Tedd's excellent teaching rightly corrected my military approach to raising our kids by the law and instead helped us to address our children's hearts. Tedd's book also injected an emphasis on grace and a critical gospel component to our parenting. But what Tripp's book could not do—what no book or method could do—was to prepare us for the trials God had planned for us to go through. God wasn't just after the hearts of our children; he was after our hearts too.

At the time, we thought our hearts were fine. We did our best to use the wisdom gathered from the many books we read to trial-proof our parenting. So we decided early on to home-school our children, since that would give us more hours each day to disciple our kids. We regulated their intake of popular culture, not allowing them to watch a ton of television. We monitored their choice of friends, but we were not prudish. We encouraged our kids to read and didn't ban popular fiction books. Our kids participated in our church home-schooling ministry, growing up in a class of more than a dozen other homeschooled kids, so they were not isolated. We are a close family and have enjoyed adventurous times away, like camping in the wilderness. Life was simple back then: we had flip phones but no tablets. Dial-up internet ran so slowly that downloading inappropriate images was next to impossible. We held consistent family devotions—in fact, I wrote a book on family devotions. As far as we could tell, we were doing every-thing right to ensure that our kids would grow up to be solid, strong Christians. Many of our friends did the same.

But then it happened—God allowed a trial to upset our utopia. I remember as if it were yesterday the call from the police, asking me to pick up my eldest son at the station. Who was he arrested with? Another church kid. Though I had done many things right, God had a tender lesson in humility and dependence planned especially for me. I will never forget the encouragement the Lord gave me in the midst of those difficult days: "I don't want you parenting standing up; I want you par-enting kneeling down."

In the moments of my greatest trial, I required a bit of *Parenting First Aid*. I needed to steep my soul in the warm bath of God's Word and refocus on what truly mattered. I needed to draw near to God and rest secure in the palm of his hand,

and to be bandaged up through the comforting ministry of his Holy Spirit.

Today, raising children hasn't gotten any easier. We now have smartphones and tablets, transgender bathrooms in department stores, two hundred more TV channels, porn images downloading in an instant and text messages that disappear with no record of their existence. Parenting is a fierce battle these days, and I see more and more wounded in the fight. I hear desperate casualties crying, "Medic! Medic!" all around me.

I've written *Parenting First Aid* as a wartime medical kit for parents in the thick of the battle. I'm not talking Band-Aids and aspirin; this kit has plasma, sutures, and splints. The goal is to encourage your soul with the Scriptures, to help you gain strength to trust in a God who can capture the heart of the most rebellious son or daughter, and to help you through the most heart-rending parenting situations.

Among the greatest threats we face as believers are the lies that the devil throws at us day and night amid our troubles. It's a struggle to find fresh faith to make it through. The apostle John, describing the success of the saints in Revelation, tells us that they conquered the accuser of the brothers by "the blood of the Lamb and by the word of their testimony" (Revelation 12:11). To help you do the same, I've included gospel-rich devotions augmented by real-life testimonies that will help you cling to hope and remind you of God's faithfulness in your parenting storm.

If you are early in your parenting journey, read this book. Utilize the Scripture it contains to strengthen your faith for the trials that are sure to come. Whether you realize it or not, parenting is a battle, and God means to prepare you to fight with faith. If you're coming to this book mid-battle, *Parenting First Aid* will help keep you in the fight, trusting God for the lives of your children. For those broken from the fight, struggling to hold on, let me encourage you with this: there is one word that, more than any other, strengthens soldiers to keep fighting. That word is "reinforcements"! The sight of fresh troops pouring onto the battlefield to help hold the line encourages the weariest soldier to keep fighting to the finish.

Some may ask, "But what if my children never turn to God?" While Scripture doesn't guarantee that every child of every believer will turn from their sin and trust in the Lord, it does encourage us to trust God and his power to save. In spite of our own parenting failures and our children's rebellion, we must never give up hope that our merciful God has a plan to reach our children by his Spirit. The goal of this devotional is to strengthen you to persevere for as long as it takes for God to rescue your children. Stand strong, never give up hope, and know that God is able to save.

Each chapter begins with a creative illustration to start off the week. This is followed by three devotions. Plan to cover a chapter per week. Do the first devotion on day one, then take time the next day to consider the questions and assignments that follow. So, if you read the assigned Scripture passage and commentary from the first devotion on Monday, take time Tuesday to answer the questions. Read the next passage and commentary on Wednesday and answer the questions on Thursday. Repeat this pattern on Friday and Saturday and read "Real Life" story on Sunday, day seven. This slower, more contemplative pace gives you a full week of material. You can, of course, go through the material at a faster pace and read a new Bible passage each day. If you take it slow, the twenty chapters will take four or five months to finish. If you read a new passage each day, you will finish in two months. Keep a journal as you go and use it to write out your answers to the questions and assignments. If you also write out your prayers for your children, you'll have a wonderful record of God's faithfulness as he answers.

The Spirit of God working through the Word is ready to reinforce our efforts. So take the next few months and soak in the encouragement of God's Word. Draw your confidence not from your own ability to parent, but from God's ability to save, his power to transform, and his willingness to help. Your reinforcements have arrived and you couldn't have a stronger Partner in the battle!

CHAPTER 1

God Planned Your Family

Psalm 139

Introduction to the Week

No matter what you are going through as a parent, you are not alone. God is with you. Most Christian parents believe this, and yet trials that weigh upon us can cause us to doubt. We do well when life is running smoothly, but when we face a trial that doesn't go away, it tests the strength of our trust in God. We thought God was there to help us, but when our prayers seem to go unanswered, we are not so sure. The Enemy is all too eager to whisper his lies in times of doubt to discourage us—"God is not with you. He is not in control, and you are on your own." Our doubts and the temptations of the devil draw our gaze away from God and onto our present challenges. We fight back with renewed prayer, but if our trials persist, we can buckle under their weight and succumb to the hopeless conclusion that we are alone in our struggle. God has done all that he can but is powerless to help us, or worse: he doesn't care.

How do we combat this problem and regain the high ground of faith? The answer is simple: we must fight lies with the truth of God's Word. Now, that may sound like the "proper" Christian answer to the problem, but the fact is that it's the only answer. If you are tempted to think, *I've tried it before and it didn't work*, dive in and give it another try.

God is our only hope and our only help, and he's written a book full of encouragements to bandage our parenting soul. There is no better place to begin than in the book of Psalms. David, the writer of most of the psalms, experienced great trials in his life and wrote many of them as his cry to God for help. During one of his struggles, David cried out to God with the words of Psalm 139, sharing fundamental truths that are preserved for us to read. They serve as an anchor for our parenting souls. God is always present, he is in complete control, and he alone can deliver us.

Day One

God Is with You

> O LORD, you have searched me and known me! You know when I sit down and when I rise up; you discern my thoughts from afar. You search out my path and my lying down and are acquainted with all my ways. Even before a word is on my tongue, behold, O LORD, you know it altogether. You hem me in, behind and before, and lay your hand upon me. Such knowledge is too wonderful for me; it is high; I cannot attain it.
>
> Where shall I go from your Spirit? Or where shall I flee from your presence? If I ascend to heaven, you are there! If I make my bed in Sheol, you are there! If I take the wings of the morning and dwell in the uttermost parts of the sea, even there your hand shall lead me, and your right hand shall hold me. If I say, "Surely the darkness shall cover me, and the

light about me be night," even the darkness is not dark to you; the night is bright as the day, for darkness is as light with you. (Psalm 139:1–12)

Ponder Anew

Soak in the reality that God is with you. He knows everything about your current situation. Not only that, God knows everything about everyone, all at the same time. God is interacting with the thoughts and intentions of every one of the more than seven billion people on the earth, all at the same time. Scripture tells us that his understanding is infinite (Psalm 147:5). He searches all hearts and knows the intent of our thoughts (1 Chronicles 28:9), and has numbered the very hairs of our heads (Matthew 10:30).

If you ask them, most Christians will assent to the belief that God is omnipresent (that is, he is fully present everywhere, all the time). But secretly, they doubt God's presence in one place—their own life. "God is everywhere else, but not with me." We have the audacity to say that God is everywhere but then doubt that he is present with us in our trial. Isn't it crazy how our sinful pride works? Satan is ever eager to sow his temptations in the field of our doubts.

The place to begin winning the war against our pride and Satan's lies is to review the truth of the psalmist and *believe*. Put your faith in God and breathe the free air again. Let the dark clouds of despair lift from around you; dare to believe that God is present and that he loves and cares for you. David isn't describing a distant, uncaring God. Instead, we see the tenderness of God as our parent, watching over our shoulder, hemming us in so that we do not stumble into dangers greater than we can handle.

The truth, "Even before a word is on my tongue, behold, O LORD, you know it altogether," is echoed by Jesus when he taught the disciples how to pray. Jesus told them not to be like the Gentiles who "heap up empty phrases," for your "Father knows what you need before you ask him" (Matthew 6:7–8). From there Jesus goes on to teach his disciples the Lord's Prayer. One of its most amazing features is its shortness. God is near his children and we can be confident that he hears our simplest prayers.

While we lift up our children to God in prayer day by day, a prayer for help in time of need can be as short as "Deliver me from evil and supply my daily bread." God knows what you need because he is with you in your struggle, patiently waiting for you to call upon him.

Bring It Home

- Which truth in Psalm 139:1–12 is hardest for you to believe—that God is all-present, that he knows your situation, or that he cares for you?
- What is most encouraging to you from this psalm?
- Reread Psalm 139:1–12 out loud as your prayer to God. As you read each phrase, make it your own and purpose to believe it in your heart.

Day Two

God Is in Complete Control

> For you formed my inward parts; you knitted me together in my mother's womb. I praise you, for I am fearfully and wonderfully made. Wonderful are your works; my soul knows it very well. My frame was not hidden from you, when I was being made in secret, intricately woven in the depths of the earth. Your eyes saw my unformed substance; in your book

were written, every one of them, the days that were formed for me, when as yet there was none of them. (Psalm 139:13–16)

Ponder Anew

Life began for each of our children at conception. You may think that I am referring to the exact moment of fertilization—the moment God began knitting together each our children within the womb. But that is not the conception to which the psalmist refers. He takes us back much further. Life began for each of our children in the mind of God, when he conceived of them and recorded their days in his book. God is so powerful that his determination of the future conception of a child results in that child's certain future. There has never been a single child that God determined to create that he failed to deliver. So, when you hear someone say that life begins at conception, remember that life began in the mind of God when, in his sovereign control, he planned each of our days and the days of every one of our children.

Still, it can be difficult to discern what God is doing with our lives. Many of our days don't seem well-planned at all. When life's trials crash in, it feels very much as though God has lost control of his broken world. But he has not lost control. We see things from the perspective of our temporal reality and we are influenced by our present needs. But God is not limited to our reality. He knows the end from the beginning. He uses the trials and difficulties to shape us like clay on a potter's wheel.

There is much we can learn about God's handiwork by watching a potter slam his clay down upon the wedging table, crushing it. Then, after slicing the clay and stacking the two pieces, he thrusts it down, so that the two are crushed together again. Over and over he repeats the process to ensure that the clay's moisture content, color, and texture are uniform. Why is this apparent violence done to the clay? To prepare it for a second, greater trial of fire that it must endure to become a useful vessel, strong and finely decorated with a glossy glaze, reflecting the beauty of its creator. So too does God work the trials of our lives for his greater purpose, that we too might reflect his glory.

The apostle Peter, who was well acquainted with trials, said, "Beloved, do not be surprised at the fiery trial when it comes upon you to test you, as though something strange were happening to you" (1 Peter 4:12). Peter said that our present trials are necessary "so that the tested genuineness of your faith—more precious than gold that perishes though it is tested by fire—may be found to result in praise and glory and honor at the revelation of Jesus Christ" (1 Peter 1:7).

As parents, we loathe life's trials. We rightly seek to safeguard our children. We childproof our homes and encourage them to wear helmets when they ride their bicycles. But no helmet can protect them from sinful hearts bent on destroying themselves, nor can we childproof their entire universe to hold back every serious life threat. Difficult trials that are hard even to mention—a sudden illness, abuse by a friend or family member, a marriage breakup that leaves your children caught between two households, a strong-willed child who grows up to reject your instruction and run away, the list of hardships goes on and on. Yet we must not fear. Whether you are currently enduring a difficult trial or you are trying to prepare yourself for a possible future challenge, Psalm 139 is like gold in those situations. If we remember that God is in control and that every one of your children's days were known to God before one of them came to be, we can find rest in the midst of the storm. It surely has its appointed end.

Knowing that God is in control may not lessen the trial. But it can give us the confidence to pray. If you are going through a trial, cry out to God for help, knowing that he is the Sovereign Lord over all. If you are reading this and you are not yet in a trial, ask God to help you when the next one comes along.

Bring It Home

- How can we find comfort in knowing that God planned every one of our days and they are written in his book?
- How have you seen God use the trials of your life for your good? How have they shaped you?
- How can Peter's encouragement in 1 Peter encourage us when we find ourselves in a fiery trial? (Answer the question and then look up Peter's encouragement in 1 Peter 1:8–9.)

Day Three

God Is Our Deliverer

> How precious to me are your thoughts, O God! How vast is the sum of them! If I would count them, they are more than the sand. I awake, and I am still with you.
>
> Oh that you would slay the wicked, O God! O men of blood, depart from me! They speak against you with malicious intent; your enemies take your name in vain. Do I not hate those who hate you, O Lord? And do I not loathe those who rise up against you? I hate them with complete hatred; I count them my enemies.
>
> Search me, O God, and know my heart! Try me and know my thoughts! And see if there be any grievous way in me, and lead me in the way everlasting! (Psalm 139:17–24)

Ponder Anew

To this point, we've discussed God's complete control over all things. We've touched upon some of God's most amazing attributes. God is omniscient (all-knowing); he knows all of our days—in fact, he knows every day of every person who ever lived and he saw those days before he created the world. We also reviewed his omnipotence (his unlimited power) as revealed in his ability to execute his plan. His plan never fails and he can work even fiery trials for our good. That leads us to the conclusion that he must be omnipresent (all-present everywhere) for he works across the world in everyone's lives at the same time. Isn't it good to know that we do not need to take turns to access God? It is not David alone who has a unique hotline to heaven. God can help you too.

If the idea that you have access to the almighty, omniscient, omnipresent Creator of the universe is difficult to comprehend, you are not alone! That is David's response too. We saw it first in verse 6, "Such knowledge is too wonderful for me; it is high; I cannot attain it." And now we see it again in verse 17, "How precious to me are your thoughts, O God! How vast is the sum of them! If I would count them, they are more than the sand." We can no sooner count the sand than fully comprehend our God. But aren't you glad that your God is that big—too big to comprehend, bigger than your problems?

After admitting that God is beyond his ability to understand, David turns the corner and cries out to his all-powerful God for deliverance. It is enough to know that he is bigger than our trials; our difficulties are not beyond his capacity to transform. With these words, "Oh that you would slay the wicked" (v. 19), David called upon God to war against the evil at work in the trials of his life. What a joy to be able to call upon the same unfathomable God, who is all-knowing, all-present, and all-powerful to deliver us from the evil that presses in. Elsewhere, David prayed, "Arise, O Lord! Save me, O my God! For you strike all my enemies on the cheek; you break the teeth of the wicked" (Psalm 3:7). That is a great prayer to add to your daily prayer list!

It is important to remember that David doesn't have a personal vendetta against a particular person. He appeals to the heart of God to judge the evil that stands against God's purpose. David writes in Psalm 69:9, "Zeal for your house has consumed me, and the reproaches of those who reproach you have fallen on me." When we as parents discern the evil and wickedness pressing against our children, we can look to David's prayer as a model for our own and call out to God to move, knowing that he is a holy God who will judge and punish sin (Romans 1:18) and bring all wickedness to an end (Malachi 4:1–3).

Finally, David invites God to search his heart (Psalm 139:23). He bows his knee to his all-powerful God. When he humbly says, "Lead me," David surrendered any argument against God and admitted his need for God's help in his fight. There is no more precious outcome to a trial than when it brings us to a place of surrender and trust in our good and gracious God. A newborn child may fight against his mother's breast and may need at times to be forced to open his mouth, only to discover that this intrusion into his personal space is meant to supply the nutrition he needs. But oh how satisfied he becomes with a full belly of fresh milk! In the same way, God uses trials to teach us to depend on him, a topic we'll return to frequently in these devotions.

So by faith, we surrender to our God—a God so vast and mighty that we might sooner count the grains of sand than plumb the depths of his nature or fully understand his plan for our lives. But by faith we trust, knowing that God is good, and all that he brings us is for our good. We, like David, bow our knee and pray, "Lead me in the way everlasting."

Bring It Home

- Where is it most difficult for you to trust God right now?
- Who are the enemies you need God to conquer?
- Cry out to God in prayer and ask him to search your heart, to show you any areas of sin that stand in the way of his plan for your life. Ask him to lead you in the way everlasting.

Real Life

My wife, Lois, came from a family of six children. I grew up with two brothers and two sisters, a sibling group of five. So it was natural that we both wanted a larger family. Lois was twenty-seven when we got married, which made us eager to start trying for children within a year of our wedding. A year later, with no baby announcement to offer our eager parents, we began to wonder if something was wrong. Several trips to the doctor and a battery of tests failed to uncover a single problem. That seemed like good news but it couldn't erase our doubts. If there was nothing medically wrong, why couldn't we conceive? Only God knew.

We buckled down in prayer and, while doing so, received the distinct impression that we were supposed to pray for twins. Lois's grandmother gave birth to twins, and they say twins skip a generation. But more than that, it felt like God commissioned us to ask for two. Still, it became increasingly difficult for my wife to share the news, "My period came today." She did so through tears. We counted days, took her temperature, charted data, and sought to time things just right, but without success for three long years.

It wasn't easy celebrating our friends' baby announcements, baby showers, and baby pictures. It was particularly challenging for Lois, who was tempted to think it was her fault. She clung to the stories in Scripture of God healing the barren woman, and we just kept praying, "God, give us twins."

Then one day Lois's period was late, and I was off to the drugstore to purchase a pregnancy test. Somewhere in the Pocono Mountains of Pennsylvania (we were tent camping), a double pink line appeared in the stick's oval window. We rejoiced, and Lois called the doctor to set up an appointment for an eight-week ultrasound. Since we had taken so long to conceive, the doctor wanted to get a look at our "pregnancy" to ensure it was a "healthy one." Now that my wife was expecting, a whole new set of fears flooded my mind. *What if the baby isn't healthy? What if the doctor can't find a heartbeat? What if it's not twins?*

Ever since the first thought came to pray for twins, Lois and I had faithfully asked God for two. In an accountability group with my fellow pastors, we filled out a sheet with our prayer requests and life goals. Each month under "family" I wrote, "Pray for twins." So as we drove to our appointment, I began a conversation. "We need to be grateful if the doctor tells us we are only having one." Lois agreed and we prepared our hearts for the strange disappointment of hearing the doctor say "your baby" singular.

After we checked in, the doctor ushered us into the ultrasound room. The technician had not yet arrived but our doctor, eager to get started, sat down next to my wife and turned on the machine. Within a few seconds, an image popped up of a blinking white dot in the middle of an inch-long oval. "There it is, a healthy pregnancy," the doctor announced with a smile on his face. Lois and I both silently prayed, "Thank you for the one."

Just then the technician burst through the door and protested as she observed the doctor in her chair. "Hey, what are you doing? You are doing my job. I guess I'm not needed anymore!"

"No, no, I only turned the machine on," the doctor replied. "You're the only one who can focus this thing and get the measurements." The woman moved the wand around, tweaked a few knobs and soon a second oval appeared on the screen next to the first.

"This is why you need me," the tech reported, pointing at the screen. "You're not having one, you are having two." Instantly, Lois and I erupted in excitement, our rejoicing changing from a silent "Thank you for the one," to shouting, "We're having twins, we're having twins!" As we both celebrated out loud, the doctor and the tech confused our rejoicing for hysterics and began to assure us that everything would be okay. "Plenty of people have had twins and survived. You are going to be okay," they said to calm us.

After we quieted down and explained the reason for our celebration, we left for home, filled with joy. At that moment, we felt blessed by the gift of twins, but our journey raising those two kids wasn't always easy. The challenges we faced helped us appreciate that we were not parenting alone. God was helping us build our house.

CHAPTER 2

Never Give Up

Galatians 6:7–10

Introduction to the Week

There is no better example of dogged determination than the hundreds of thousands of attempts Dude Perfect has logged making their trick shot videos. If you haven't logged on to watch these five young guys shoot basketballs, join their 3.2 billion views: go to www.dudeperfect.com and become their 3.2 billion-and-one viewer. It all started with a "bet you can't do this" challenge for a free sandwich; it's now an internet sensation, garnering endorsements from major corporate sponsors and the attention of some serious professional athletes.

They've made basketball shots from the tops of stadiums, out of the Goodyear Blimp, over jet airliners, and with giant slingshots. They have hit moving basketball hoops on the backs of trucks from crazy distances. Go on their website and you'll see that they give the glory to God, saying, "We believe that nothing happens by accident, that God's given us this platform for a reason, and that we have an opportunity to make an impact on the lives of countless others all around the globe. Above all else, our ultimate goal is to glorify Jesus Christ in everything we do. We want to use this platform for something much bigger than us."

They hold the world record for the longest basketball shot—533 feet from the top of a sky scraper. How do they do it? They just never give up. They keep trying and trying and trying. While they set the standard for internet trick shots, they illustrate an important biblical principle: never give up.

Toward the end of his letter to the Galatians, the apostle Paul exhorted the Christians in Galatia to never give up. While his encouragement was not designed for parents specifically, there are few more encouraging verses to moms and dads than Galatians 6:9, which promises that we will reap a harvest if we refuse to give up doing good. Our children are like seeds. We plant them in the good soil of the gospel and water them with love and instruction. Then we depend on God to cause them to grow. Like farmers tending a field, we fight against drought, pests, weeds, and thieves all looking to destroy the harvest. All that hard work can leave the strongest parent weary. That is why it is important to remember Paul's words. This week we'll take a look at Paul's exhortation. If you are discouraged and feel like throwing in the towel, draw fresh strength from Paul's encouragement and gain the faith to tackle another day.

Day One

It Is Never Too Late to Sow Good Seed

> Do not be deceived: God is not mocked, for whatever one sows, that will he also reap. For the one who sows to his own flesh will from the flesh reap corruption, but the one who sows to the Spirit will from the Spirit reap eternal life. (Galatians 6:7–8)

Ponder Anew

Depending on how you read them, these two verses can be the most discouraging or the most encouraging words to a parent. We know that we all deserve destruction because of our sin. If God allowed any of us to reap the fruit of what we've sown in our rebellion against God, none of us could stand. The writer of Psalm 130 says it well:

> If you, LORD, kept a record of sins, Lord, who could stand? But with you there is forgiveness, so that we can, with reverence, serve you. (Psalm 130:3–4 NIV)

Notice how the writer of Psalm 130 connects God's dismissing our guilt, which seems like a miscarriage of justice, with forgiveness. Our forgiveness is only possible through the sacrifice of Jesus upon the cross; he reaped the consequences for the bad seed we have sown. This is true for the sins we've committed personally, but it is also true for our failures as parents. Jesus Christ died for our failures, that we and our families might be redeemed. So when you look at Galatians 6:7—that we reap what we sow—you need to remember that Jesus took our punishment if we are believers. Galatians isn't referring to a works-righteousness salvation. It is talking about the way we live in light of the cross. God has given us his Spirit so that we need not live as we once lived, according to the flesh. If we sow to the Spirit, we will reap eternal life. If we run to Jesus Christ by his Spirit and live for him, we reap eternal rewards.

But what about the mistakes we've all made as parents? Perhaps you're experiencing a harvest of bad fruit from past sins, and it threatens to cripple you. There are consequences to our failures, but it is important to remember this simple truth: it is never too late to plant good seed, and God is able to erase the harmful consequences of our failures. That is the core of redemption.

Condemnation seeks to immobilize us so that we become like a farmer who lost his crop, but is so discouraged that he cannot move a muscle to replant. Instead of dwelling on what you've lost, be like the farmer who throws off discouragement because he knows that there is still time to replant. If God allowed the full measure of the consequences for our sin to be visited on our children, every one of our kids would end up in prison. This is true for even the most diligent parent. But God is merciful, and it is never too late to plant good seed into our lives and the lives of our children. So turn over the soil of your own heart first and run to Jesus. Confess your sins and failings to God and experience the fruit of forgiveness. Then turn over the soil of the hearts of your children by showing them the same kind of love God has shown you. Say no to discouragement, complacency, and confess your sins, where appropriate, to your children. Start devotions again and continue planting the seeds of the gospel. By God's grace and the Spirit's help, you will see God cause the good seed of the gospel to grow, flower, and bear fruit.

Bring It Home

- Where do you find yourself struggling most with feeling condemnation as a parent? Make a list of these areas. As you do, remember that as God is at work shaping your children, he is also at work shaping your heart through parenting.
- Reflect on the gospel, that Jesus died on the cross for all of our sins and failures, taking the punishment we deserve. Then tear up your list, confessing your failures to God and asking for his cleansing forgiveness to wash away your sin.

Day Two

Do Not Grow Weary of Doing Good

> And let us not grow weary of doing good, for in due season we will reap, if we do not give up. (Galatians 6:9)

Ponder Anew

There are few more reassuring words for a parent than the encouragement found in Galatians 6:9 that we will reap a harvest. While this is not a passage specifically about parenting, the principle of trusting God and not growing weary is directly applicable to that calling. Still, as we walk through serious parenting challenges, the best of us forget Paul's promise and struggle for the faith to continue. When trials persist, the fog of doubt and unbelief rolls in and blankets us with such a cloud that we cannot see the next step ahead. Have you ever found yourself in such a place? Perhaps your child has thrown repeated tantrums and has become a terror, or you have an older child who speaks spiteful, rebellious words against you. Other parents battle for faith as they care for a chronically ill child. Some children have been exposed to serious sin, and parents feel powerless against its lasting effects. In every case, Paul's message is designed to strengthen us, calling us to "not grow weary of doing good, for in due season, we will reap."

While losing faith in such grave parenting trials seems understandable, we are too often undone by our parenting difficulties. The smallest trial will have us forget the omnipotence of our great God. A toddler who can't seem to stay in bed but leaves the bedroom a dozen times every evening can make a parent feel like giving up and letting the kids do what they want. But if we give up on such a small thing, what will we do in the midst of greater trials? The key in any parenting trial is trusting our good and faithful God. If we could fully comprehend that he is all-powerful, all-loving, and able to strengthen us and move into our situation, then we would see any trial as small compared to his greatness.

"Let us not grow weary of doing good," the apostle tells us. Like the farmer who turns over the soil, removes the rocks, and plants the good seed, we must wait for the seed we plant in our children's hearts to sprout and grow. After the seed sprouts, as the plants inch their way upward, we, like the farmer, must not grow weary in battling the weeds and pests, and work to irrigate the field during drought. What motivates the farmer and keeps him from giving up? He has faith that if he does not grow weary, he will reap a harvest in due season. The same is true for us, Paul exhorts us.

Now, God does not guarantee that the harvest will come in four months, like a farmer's typical growing season. Our season of cultivation and care is often much longer. What if, in God's design, the due season he planned for us is not four months, but four years or more? What if the season he has charted out for us is our entire lives? Is it then okay to give up?

We only give up because we start to believe that there will be no harvest, no good fruit for our labors. While God does not promise us that our harvest will come within a particular timeframe, he does tell us that the harvest will come. That is where the promise from today's verse is designed to strengthen us. We do not know the length of our "due season," but we have this promise: "We will reap." No person serving God until the end of their days will be without a harvest to show for their labors. Remember this: You are not responsible for creating the good fruit; you are responsible for continuing to sow the seed. So, do not grow weary in doing good and do not stop in the fight for your kids. Keep sowing, for in due season you shall reap.

Bring It Home

- Where are you most tempted to give up because you haven't seen good fruit for your efforts or prayers?
- Find a private place and cry out to God for strength. Sometimes the best way to pray in the midst of trials is to call out loud. Speak out to God and reaffirm your trust in his ability to produce a harvest from your efforts.
- Resolve to keep cultivating the soil of your children's hearts while you trust God for the results.

Day Three

God's People Are Called to Help One Another

> So then, as we have opportunity, let us do good to everyone, and especially to those who are of the household of faith. (Galatians 6:10)

Ponder Anew

There is an unspoken rule in the farming community; farmers help farmers. The Amish community exemplifies this through their tradition of barn raisings. While the materials needed to build a barn are expensive, paying for the labor to construct it can triple the cost. In a barn raising, all the men in the community are expected to help with the construction. Imagine how encouraged the recipient family is to see the structure rise in a day and completed in two!

While instructing and caring for children are the responsibilities of the parent, raising children is also the responsibility of the whole church community. Asaph spoke of the corporate responsibility for the next generation in Psalm 78 when he said, "We will tell the next generation the praiseworthy deeds of the LORD, his power, and the wonders he has done" (Psalm 78:4 NIV). The operative word is "we." We have a responsibility to reach the coming generation. Raising children is a task far greater than any one parent can handle. Like a barn raising, it requires the whole community. Just like farmers help one another, Christian parents help other Christian parents.

One of the best ways to help another Christian parent is to share your current struggles with believers in your circle of friendships. The Enemy is quick to convince us that we are alone in our struggles, but our sin and sin-related struggles are not unique (1 Corinthians 10:13). The difficulties we face in parenting are common. Too often parents struggle privately with the same challenges, secretly thinking that everyone else in the group enjoys a perfect home. By sharing your challenges, you open the door for others to help and for real, open, discussion to begin within your circle of friends. When others share a difficulty, be sure to encourage them and look for ways to do good to them. But if you keep your struggle to yourself, you become like a farmer who tries to raise his own barn, without the help of his community. It doesn't take long for discouragement to set in.

Paul understood our need to encourage one another as we live out the Christian life. He knew the difference an encouraging word or deed could have on a person in difficulty. Paul thanked the Philippians for their help in his time of need in prison, which encouraged him deeply. Consider his words and imagine that he was thanking them for their support through a trial with a rebellious child.

> I thank my God in all my remembrance of you, always in every prayer of mine for you all making my prayer with joy, because of your partnership in the gospel from the first day until now. And I am sure of this, that he who began a good work in you will bring

it to completion at the day of Jesus Christ. It is right
for me to feel this way about you all, because I hold
you in my heart, for you are all partakers with me of
grace, both in my imprisonment and in the defense
and confirmation of the gospel. (Philippians 1:3–7)

Let's open up with one another and seek to do good to
those who are laboring to sow and not give up within the
household of faith.

Bring It Home

- Why do we hesitate to share our struggles with others?
  What excuses do you typically make for keeping your
  challenges to yourself?
- Are you keeping your struggles hidden from those
  around you? Who are the people God wants you to share
  your trials with and ask for advice and prayer?
- Think of three parents you could seek to encourage.
  (One sure way is to take a week to pray for them and
  then send an encouraging note to let them know that
  you did. Mention specific prayers so that your encouragement will sink deeply into their souls.)

Real Life

Oma Petz ("Oma" means "grandmother" in German) was
eighty years old when she told my wife and me this story from
her childhood. She still remembered the terrifying moments
and her uncle's frantic plea as though it happened yesterday.

Heinrich Petz lived with his wife, Ida, and their family in
a farmhouse he built for them by hand. Late one evening, the
entire household, including a young Jewish girl who was staying with them, was awakened from a deep sleep by an uncle's
heavy pounding on their front door.

"He told us, 'Move quickly; you must leave now. Take only what you can carry.' We grabbed what we could and climbed into his wagon, not knowing where we were going." The Second World War had finally intruded upon their lives.

When it was safe, Oma's family, along with their young Jewish boarder, returned to their farm to discover a pile of rubble where their stone farmhouse once stood. Shocked by their enormous loss, Heinrich gathered the family to encourage their flagging faith, "We may have lost everything, but we have not lost Jesus," he said. Then he led them in a prayer, thanking God for protecting them and asking the Lord for help and provision. With no place to go, the family slept among the stones that once made up their home.

A few days later, their Jewish houseguest spotted the silhouette of a man rounding a distant hill and immediately recognized his gait. "Papa!" she shouted, and ran to his arms. After hearing how the family had cared for his daughter, the wealthy businessman's heart swelled with thanks. He said to Heinrich, "I will rebuild your home." He smiled, adding, "On one condition, that you allow my daughter to continue living with you." God had answered their prayer in a matter of days.

The Petz family rebuilt their home, but soon they were once again forced to leave the farmhouse. This time they were displaced by German troops seeking to billet there. Weeks later, when the soldiers left, the family was allowed to reclaim their property. Supplies were gone and the house left a mess, but nothing a week's work couldn't remedy. Later, they were forced out of their home a third and final time and bounced from farm to farm. Most families treated them kindly, but some did no more than toss them a few potatoes.

When WWII ended, they were left homeless because their property was taken from them. Once again Oma remembered her father gathering the family close with the same message: "We may have lost everything, but we have not lost Jesus."

Destitute, Heinrich and Ida sent out letters to every distant friend and relation, some in the United States, asking for help.

That was when my wife's grandfather, Carl Rausch, got involved. Concerned about German Christians left destitute after the war, he sponsored them to come to the United States. Carl employed the men in his machine shop in New Haven, Connecticut, and welcomed the Petz family into his own home.

I left our time with Oma grateful for Carl's generosity but even more amazed by Heinrich's faith. Heinrich himself never made it out of Germany, but the prayer he offered in their darkest hour, "We may have lost everything, but we have not lost Jesus," was forever etched upon Oma's heart. Despite losing everything several times over, Heinrich never gave up. He trusted Jesus through it all and in his due season he reaped a wonderful harvest—children, grandchildren, great-grandchildren, and even great-great-grandchildren who love the Lord.

CHAPTER 3

Consider the Lilies
Matthew 6:25-34

Introduction to the Week

Have you heard the old story about the man who worried himself to death? "Frank" worked in a railroad yard repairing box cars. At the end of a long day, while inspecting the inside of large box car, he was accidentally locked in. Frank screamed and pounded on the door, worried that he would suffocate if not rescued, but no one heard his cries.

The next day, when the boxcar was opened to load it, workers discovered Frank's body and a message scrawled into the wooden floor: "I couldn't breathe and ran out of air." Autopsy reports determined that the cause of death was suffocation, even though there were plenty of gaps in the door for air to circulate. Frank had been so worried about suffocating that he did!

This story is fiction, but it's true that worry and anxiety affect our emotional state and our behavior. The person who worries that he won't get enough rest before a big test ends up spending half the night anxiously trying to go to sleep. The marksman who is anxious about the loud blast of his gun flinches just before pulling the trigger, sending his round off target. The pitcher who is so concerned about walking a man in with bases loaded can't throw a strike to save his life.

But there is one area of worry that seems to eclipse them all: worrying about our children if they are sick or struggling. This week we'll review what Jesus taught about worry and apply what we learn to our challenges as parents.

Day One

Worry Doesn't Help

> "Therefore I tell you, do not be anxious about your life, what you will eat or what you will drink, nor about your body, what you will put on. Is not life more than food, and the body more than clothing? Look at the birds of the air: they neither sow nor reap nor gather into barns, and yet your heavenly Father feeds them. Are you not of more value than they? And which of you by being anxious can add a single hour to his span of life? And why are you anxious about clothing? Consider the lilies of the field, how they grow: they neither toil nor spin, yet I tell you, even Solomon in all his glory was not arrayed like one of these. But if God so clothes the grass of the field, which today is alive and tomorrow is thrown into the oven, will he not much more clothe you, O you of little faith?" (Matthew 6:25–30)

Ponder Anew

Jesus's teaching on worry comes at the end of a discussion about choosing heavenly treasure over earthly treasure and living for God, not money. The immediate application of his teaching is to our concern with material provision, the food and clothing we need daily, but the fundamental truths of this message apply beyond our requirements for basic life necessities.

For example, we can apply this passage to parenting and find encouragement not to worry when it comes to our children. After all, if God cares so much about providing for the grass of the field and the birds of the air, how much more will he provide for you in your parenting? And if God is willing to provide the food and clothing we need, surely he would not abandon us in our efforts to care for and lead our children. No, the same character of God that eagerly provides food and clothing for his people will provide for us in parenting our children as well.

Earlier in the chapter (Matthew 6:7–13), Jesus introduced his disciples to the amazing truth that God is our Father. We can pray to him for our daily needs, ask for his kingdom to come, and for deliverance from evil. He gives us prayer as the way to deal with our worry. We can ask God to push back the forces of evil that have aligned themselves against his kingdom in our lives. We know that one day God will fully restore his kingdom and there will be no more evil, sickness, or suffering. By asking God for his help, we are asking him to apply some of that end-time restoration to our present situation.

Another fundamental truth from this passage that applies to parenting comes in the form of a question: "Which of you by being anxious can add a single hour to his span of life?" (v. 27). With this inquiry, Jesus is laying the choice before us: we can address our trials through worry, which gives us nothing, or place our trust in our heavenly Father, who is eager to provide. Far from adding days to our lives, worry steals them, robbing us of sleep and peace. Did you ever notice how worry loves to focus on the most terrible of outcomes? Faith, demonstrated through prayer, trusts God to answer the challenges we face in our family, whether it is a sick child, a rebellious son or daughter, or any other difficulty.

Finally, in verse 30, the reason for our worry is revealed— a lack of faith. Faith reminds us of God's past faithfulness (both in Scripture and in our previous experience) to assure us of his present faithfulness, for God doesn't change. If we could trust God before, we can trust him now. We have a heavenly Father who is eager to hear our prayers. If we are more valuable to him than the grass of the field, for which he faithfully provides flowers, how much more should we expect him to provide for us?

Bring It Home

- Where are you most prone to worry when it comes to your family? Is it for your material provision or do you worry about the health, welfare, or souls of your children?
- Where do you see a lack of faith for what God can or will do in your situation? What does it look like to repent of unbelief and start trusting God again?
- How has worry robbed you of days?

Day Two

God Knows What You Need

"Therefore do not be anxious, saying, 'What shall we eat?' or 'What shall we drink?' or 'What shall we wear?' For the Gentiles seek after all these things, and your heavenly Father knows that you need them all. But seek first the kingdom of God and his righteousness, and all these things will be added to you." (Matthew 6:31–33)

Ponder Anew

Did you ever realize that fear, worry, and anxiety force questions upon you? These questions often begin with "What if." "What if they start . . . ?" "What if they get into . . . ?" If we analyze these questions that come to tempt us, we often discover that unbelief lurks just below the surface, stealing our peace and breeding a mistrust of God. Once we lose faith in God, we complain and blame him as the cause of our trials instead of the help we need to resolve them.

In introducing these questions ("What shall we eat?" or "What shall we drink?" or "What shall we wear?"), Jesus is pointing us back to the unbelief Israel exhibited during their deliverance from Egypt. It wasn't long after Israel escaped Pharaoh that God intentionally led them into a trap at the Red Sea, so that he might demonstrate his faithfulness (Exodus 14:1–4). When the armies of Egypt pursued them and cornered them against the sea, the people questioned God. "'Is it because there are no graves in Egypt that you have taken us away to die in the wilderness? What have you done to us in bringing us out of Egypt?'" (Exodus 14:11).

God delivered Israel that day by opening up the Red Sea. They crossed over on dry ground and when Pharaoh pursued them, the walls of the sea collapsed upon the Egyptians, giving God glory over Pharaoh. The people of Israel danced and rejoiced, singing, "The LORD is my strength and my song, and he has become my salvation" (Exodus 15:2). But it didn't take long for those same people to forget God's salvation and to fear and question, "What shall we drink?" Their praise to God for his deliverance ends in Exodus 15:21 and their questions to God about water begin three verses later. Nine verses later, they are questioning God about food.

We are just like the Israelites. We forget the amazing salvation God provided through the cross. Anxiety grips us and, like the Israelites, we question God's faithfulness to provide. God knew that the Israelites needed food and water and he knows that we need them as well. He calls us to trust that he will amply provide for our needs. Instead of questioning God's faithfulness or complaining about the trial, we should trust God and watch him provide.

Parenting provides any number of opportunities to trust in God. Looking back at Israel, it is easy to see that all they needed to do was ask. "Hey Moses, would you ask our generous God to provide us a bit of water to drink as we travel?" Remember, God went before Israel as a pillar of cloud by day and fire by night. They knew that he was with them; all they had to do was ask, and then continue the mission, knowing that he would take care of them.

God has delivered us from Egypt (our sinful lives as unbelievers) and is leading us to the Promised Land (heaven with Jesus in a re-created new heavens and earth). While we journey through the wilderness between the two, we need not question God. We can ask him in prayer to provide—even if our need appears as impossible and overwhelming as the Red Sea.

Bring It Home

- List all the ways God has answered your prayers in the past. How can reviewing this list strengthen your faith for the current challenges you face?
- How is our salvation in Christ like the salvation God provided for Israel in opening up the Red Sea?
- How is our complaining similar to Israel's, who quickly forgot God's past deliverance to worry about their present difficulty?

Day Three

Today Has Enough Trouble

"Therefore do not be anxious about tomorrow, for tomorrow will be anxious for itself. Sufficient for the day is its own trouble." (Matthew 6:34)

While we should not worry about tomorrow and what hasn't yet taken place, it is completely understandable that we are concerned about today and our immediate troubles. God is not saying that it is okay to give ourselves over to worry, but he is sympathetic to the fact that we've got to work through the challenges we face daily. Consider this analogy: It does you no good to worry about your water heater, fearing that it will spring a leak one day, but you do need to "worry" if it is currently leaking water onto your floor. Today has enough troubles of its own.

Raising kids provides you with enough worries for the day—just getting them up and out of the house on time for school is a small miracle. Getting them to complete their homework—or even accurately disclose what homework they have—is enough to worry about, let alone start thinking about all the trouble they might get into weeks, months, or even years down the road. The Enemy is ever ready to tempt us to fear the worst outcome and then worry as if our life depends on it!

Then there are the real troubles that confront you, such as the child who was scheduled to get home at 9 p.m. but is still out of touch at 10 p.m. We still need to trust God and pray, but concern over your child's whereabouts is completely understandable. Where we get into trouble is when we allow our concern over the present situation to bleed into worry about tomorrow. What if they don't come home tonight? What if this is only the beginning of a downward spiral? Fear is ever ready to take the reins and banish faith, tempting us to extend today's concerns into fears about tomorrow.

There is no need to worry about tomorrow's troubles, which may or may not happen. You have enough to pray about with the situations that confront you right now.

Bring It Home

- List your worries on paper in two columns. In the first column, write out the troubles you are experiencing right now. In the second column, write down your worries for tomorrow. Cut the paper in half, tear up the tomorrow side, and toss it in the trash. Then spend time praying for today until God gives you peace that he is with you and will provide.
- One of the best ways to fight worry is to share our fears and concerns with others. How well are you doing in sharing your fears and asking others for prayer? Take time to call a friend and confess your unbelief, anxiety, and worry. Ask your friend to join you in prayer and hold you accountable to cast your cares upon the Lord.

Real Life

It wasn't long after we discovered that Lois was pregnant with twins that she began spotting. Soon she was on the phone with the doctor. His response confirmed our greatest fears—we may have lost one of the twins. Several days went by. The spotting continued. We arranged for a doctor's visit to see if two heartbeats could be found, indicating that both babies were yet alive.

It is in moments when you have no control and need to trust God for the outcome that worry and anxiety assault you. The "what-ifs" flood your mind. What if the doctor doesn't hear two heartbeats? What if he doesn't hear any? There was nothing we could do to change the situation, and I knew that worry could make things worse. Stress in early pregnancy is a precipitating factor in miscarriage, and nothing will stress you out more than anxious thoughts and worries, especially when there is nothing you can do.

If you are short on money to cover your bills, you can take a second job. If your family has a history of heart disease, you can at least exercise and watch what you eat. But how do you stop your body from spotting? There is nothing you can do but pray. Faith leads you to pray as your first, not last, resort, but worry tries to rob you of confidence that praying will do any good.

I couldn't allow myself to believe that God would honor our prayers for twins only to let one of the babies die. Together we prayed and trusted God for the sound of two heartbeats. During the arduous wait before the doctor's appointment, I meditated on God's faithfulness, his goodness to provide, and his answers to our prayers in the past. I also considered his sovereignty and accepted his rule and reign over our situation. Prayer gave Lois and me an answer to our anxious thoughts and worries, and faith applied to our situation enabled us to trust God no matter the outcome. Still, our footing wasn't sure. We went through those days like a mountain climber stuck on a narrow ledge without ropes, knowing that the next step could be his last, yet knowing he must step forward nonetheless.

When at last the spotting abated and the doctor confirmed two heartbeats, we experienced a measure of relief, but worry didn't throw in the towel. The battle for faith continued and the "what-ifs" launched many a counterattack. Prayer became the weapon we used as we took every foul thought captive. God answered our prayers. Lois carried the twins full-term. They were both healthy and active and we were elated, until it came time to nurse and the little kids refused.

Then the "what-ifs" driven by our worry became illogical—which is what worry does. What if our babies can't nurse? What if they don't stimulate milk production in my wife? What if they need to be tube fed? Will they ever grow up? God in his kindness wouldn't allow our fears to fester. He sent in a grandmotherly aide who volunteered for decades in the nursery. When that woman grabbed hold of our baby's head and shoved it onto my wife's breast, I thought he would suffocate! While her actions said, "Look, kid, don't give me any crap about not nursing," her voice spoke a sweet, "There you go, you can do it." When he started to suckle and then latched on, I could have danced in the room. How quickly I allowed worry to rob me of peace! Worry is like that.

Several years later, God didn't answer our prayers to preserve a child. Our fears were confirmed as we lost a son or daughter to a miscarriage. By God's grace and with his help, we decided to trust God in our grief, affirming that he is good and would one day reunite us with the child we lost. Worry tells you that the worst will happen and all will be lost. Prayer places the outcome in the hands of the Lord, who can deliver you from a trial and sustain you through grief.

CHAPTER 4

You Can't Parent Alone

Psalm 127

Introduction to the Week

A couple of summers ago, I set out to build a basic wood-shed—three walls and a pitched roof, open in front. The first step in the construction was to fix a joist across the top of the two front corner posts to support the roof in the front. Once upright and level, I'd do the same for the rear and then connect them with side rails. The whole structure looked a little like four legs of a chair with a slanted seat for a roof. All I had to do was lift the front frame in place and pound a nail through a diagonal support to hold it upright, and then do the same for the rear frame. Once the front and rear frames were held by their diagonal supports, attaching a crossbar would be relatively easy. But I soon discovered that I only had two hands.

As I lifted the heavy frame upright, I held the diagonal support up with my knee. I held a level against the beam and watched as the bubble in the tube of the level indicated that the post stood true. Two nails sat at the ready, between pursed lips. *Perfect*, I thought, keeping a close eye on the bubble. I pulled a nail from my mouth and pushed it through the pilot hole in the diagonal support, where it rested without falling out. The process went according to plan until I reached for my hammer, which sat three feet away on the ground laughing at me. Time and time again I tried but found I could not pound the nail and hold the post level. With each successive attempt, I grew more and more tired. I finally realized I could not build the woodshed on my own.

About that time, my son Noah pulled up in his car. Desperate for help, I called out to my son, who gladly held the frame in place while I secured the diagonal supports. It took seconds, and we got it right on the first try. I needed his assistance several more times in the process. The woodshed stands as a testimony that I can't build a house alone, which is one of two pictures God gives us in Psalm 127 to encourage us to ask him for help in building our family.

Day One

A Song of Solomon

A Song of Ascents. Of Solomon

Unless the LORD builds the house,
    those who build it labor in vain.
Unless the LORD watches over the city,
    the watchman stays awake in vain. (Psalm 127:1)

Ponder Anew

Psalm 127 is the only psalm attributed to Solomon. It is placed in the Psalter in the middle of a run of Psalms of Ascent. The "house" of verse 1 is the "house of the LORD" mentioned in Psalm 122:1; the city is the city of Jerusalem. But these references have broad application today. Verse 1 is often quoted and applied to the church, marriage, or even building projects. There is a universal truth captured in these verses, similar to what Jesus taught when he said, "I am the vine; you are the branches. Whoever abides in me and I in him, he it is that bears much fruit, for apart from me you can do nothing" (John 15:5). The second half of the psalm, which outlines the blessing of children, directs the application of this psalm to the family. Solomon in all his wisdom knew that God's people are made up of families. Unless the Lord is at work with you, building your household, your efforts will fall short.

The psalm begins with a parallelism, two phrases, one after the other, which teach the same truth. The second of the two statements in a parallelism brings an additional depth of understanding. Unless the Lord builds the house with you, you are going to have trouble. Not only can't you build alone, you also don't have eyes on the back of your head. At any point in time, half the city remains unguarded. Try as you might, you only have 180 degrees of sight, and the enemy loves to attack at the rear, where you can't see him coming.

Do you remember a time when you faced a large job or project, like raking a yard full of leaves or cleaning up all the Thanksgiving dishes? What a joy it is when a friend offers to help. Parenting is an insurmountable task. What a joy it is to hear God saying, "Do you need a little help?" The God who created light with a single command offers to partner with you through this parenting psalm. If King Solomon, the wisest man to ever live (apart from Jesus), knew he needed God, who are we to think otherwise? And here is the exciting part—God is willing to help us.

Psalm 127 is listed as a "Song of Ascents," a song designed to lead the congregation to worship as they ascended the hill to the temple. It is a doorway to praise. But how do we praise God during our parenting trials? There are few challenges that rob you of strength faster than a rebellious child you can't reach or a struggling child you're losing faith to help. But it's equally true that nothing can restore your joy and move you to worship more than remembering that it is not all up to you: God is the second man on your team. His Spirit fills the heart of every believer, and his presence is with you in your home. You have help—powerful help from a willing God, capable of creating light and calming your storm with a word.

Bring It Home

- Reflect on your parenting. Have much have you been trying to parent alone, apart from God?
- God loves to use parenting challenges, whether it be a rebellious child or an ailing one, to teach us the truth of Psalm 127:1–2: we must depend on him. Call out to God and invite his help. Surrender your challenging situation to him.

Day Two

The Gift of Sleep

> It is in vain that you rise up early
>   and go late to rest,
> eating the bread of anxious toil;
>   for he gives to his beloved sleep. (Psalm 127:2)

Ponder Anew

God knows that parents worry. We worry about the health of our children when they are well, and worry about their well-being when they are sick. We worry about their future—their future education, spouse, and job. We worry about their lack of faith or their turning from the Lord if they demonstrate faith. Worry is ready to rob us blind of our peace twenty-four hours a day, seven days a week.

Worry sprouts from the seeds of our doubts and fears. We doubt God's goodness or we fear he won't help us. Then we take life's challenges into our own hands. And since we are not in sovereign control over all things, our only recourse is to worry. Worry robs you of sleep on both ends of the night. You can't fall asleep for worry and as soon as you wake up, worry is ready to enslave you for another day of "anxious toil." Anxious toil is better known as spinning your wheels, trying to do what only God can do. The remedy for worry is repentance—we need to admit that we are not trusting God and to return to depending upon him in our weakness. It is in weakness that we are strong, for there God's Spirit rushes in to help us trust him with the challenges we face.

Jesus asked his disciples this question: "Which of you by being anxious can add a single hour to his span of life?" (Matthew 6:27). Now apply that to your parenting challenge: Which of you can regenerate the heart of your son or daughter by being anxious? Which of you can keep your daughter from relapsing into drug use by worry? Which of you can kill a single cancer cell that is attacking the body of your child by being anxious? None of us can. The truth is that we are weak; we can't change our circumstances and we are helpless in our trials on our own. But it is also true that God is strong, in control of all things, and committed to provide for us as a good Father. "Therefore do not be anxious . . . your heavenly Father knows that you need . . . seek first the kingdom of God and his righteousness, and all these things will be added to you" (Matthew 6:31–33).

We will find rest when we repent of our worry and call out to our trustworthy God. Our circumstances may not change, but once God is at the center of our struggle and we know he is on the job, we can rest, for he gives his beloved sleep.

So, if you struggle to fall asleep or you begin your first waking moments in worry, take a moment to drop to your knees and engage the one who is able to restore your confidence and faith.

Bring It Home

- Where do you most struggle to trust God for your children?
- Read Matthew 6:25–33. What is the Spirit of God telling you to trust the Father for?
- What does repentance from worry look like for you? Take time to confess your unbelief and ask the Spirit of God to help you rest in God's promises and what he can uniquely do.

Day Three

Children Are a Heritage

> Behold, children are a heritage from the LORD,
>   the fruit of the womb a reward.
> Like arrows in the hand of a warrior
>   are the children of one's youth.
> Blessed is the man
>   who fills his quiver with them!
> He shall not be put to shame
>   when he speaks with his enemies in the gate.
> (Psalm 127:3–5)

Ponder Anew

Our children are a heritage from the Lord. The Hebrew word translated "heritage" is often translated "inheritance" and used in association with the land God gave Israel. This inheritance, provided by God's authority and power, nevertheless had to be secured by his people (Deuteronomy 15:4; 25:19). God gave Israel the land, but they had to take possession of it, and they could not do so apart from God's enabling power. In this one word "heritage," we have both a gift and a call to take hold of it but, like Israel, we can only do so with God's help. We are back where we started. We need the assisting hand of God to build our family.

Our children are like arrows in the hands of a warrior. In war, an archer uses his arrows to reach further into the battle than he can go. Arrows fly over obstacles, penetrating deep into enemy lines. We as believers are on a mission to build the church, and God has given us children to go beyond our reach. There is a promise here that, as arrows are shot into battle, our children will join us in the mission and advance the gospel. God gives us children as blessing and reward. Long after we are gone, they will carry the gospel message to the next generation.

Perhaps it is hard for you to imagine ever sending your wayward children into battle on the Lord's behalf. That is where we must trust God's promises and do our part to keep sharing the gospel with our kids. God can use our feeble efforts to break down the walls they've erected against us and God. Israel faced insurmountable odds when God gave them the land as a heritage and told them to take possession. God could have won the victory on his own but he wanted to use Israel. When they encountered the walls of Jericho, God told them to march around the city, shout, and blow their horns, and he would do the rest. I'm sure that the guards of Jericho laughed at Israel's feeble efforts until God broke down their walls. As God broke down the walls of Jericho, so will he break the walls of rebellion surrounding the hearts of our children, using our most feeble attempts to share the gospel with them. God will use your children to advance his kingdom!

God calls us to parent, but not alone. God will help you build your house and watch over your city. He will give you rest from anxiety and he has given you your sons and daughters as arrows, meant to help secure his gospel victory.

Bring It Home

- How can remembering God's assistance in helping Israel capture the Promised Land help us as parents in our parenting challenges?
- Write out a prayer that asks God for specific help with each of your children. Use it to call out to God, with faith that he is able to move on your behalf.

Real Life

Before conceiving our twins, Lois and I were as prepared for parenting as any couple could be. We both babysat extensively and lived with Christian families. So we sat in the front row, watching others' strengths and weaknesses as parents. I read the most definitive books on parenting available at the time and planned to follow the advice each gave with the military precision I applied to the rest of my life.

As our children grew, life threw us a curveball or two. Potty training humbled me when it didn't work as I had planned. That should have been a sign that I needed God more than the parenting books. But we pressed on, purposing to be good Christian parents and expecting our children to become good Christian kids. We were careful not to expose Emma and Nathan to too much TV or inappropriate programs. They grew up with family worship and (somewhat) daily devotions. We decided to homeschool them so that we could shape their curriculum with a God-centered focus and we enrolled our twins in our local church homeschool co-op. We sat together as a family in church and looked to help all our kids develop friendships with other children from our church.

Our daughter Emma turned out just like we planned. She wasn't perfect, a bit slow to do work or chores, but she responded well to discipline and God began to draw her to himself at a young age. She gave her life to Christ in her teen years. She saw how God lifted the weight of sin from the shoulders of others in our church and, in the middle of one night, she went into the bathroom to call out to God. She wouldn't stop until he removed the weight of her sin. God kindly responded with grace, and she left the bathroom a different person. We noticed a difference in her service around the home as she started helping out without being asked. She became a shining star.

Nathan, on the other hand, played the part of a good Christian son on the outside, but inside he was far from God. A sizeable group of his homeschool classmates created an anti-fellowship pact, where they pledged they would never tell on each other, no matter what they did. So, while I slept at night, Nathan was sneaking out of our house to meet up with his other church friends to go drinking in a local park. It wasn't until another family caught one of their kids that we found out that Nathan was involved. I remember crying out to the Lord, pleading my case. "God," I prayed, "I am sleeping at two in the morning! How can I be expected to parent twenty-four hours a day?" We also told our son that he was too young to date, but that didn't stop him. He had a secret girlfriend in his double-life world. To us, she was just a "friend."

Then came the first of several run-ins with the police. I got the call no dad ever wants to receive. "Can you come pick up your son at the station?" He and his girlfriend were taken into custody since they were in a car containing drugs. I felt a wave of relief when I discovered that the police did not charge them, as the drugs belonged to the car's owner. But subsequent run-ins revealed that my son was as involved as any of his other church friends.

"Church kids!" I called out to God, laying out my case for God's unfairness to me. "Lord, we homeschooled them. We did devotions with our kids and family worship. We were careful not to expose them to worldliness, and we limited their friends to other church kids. What more are we supposed to do?"

At that moment God was kind to answer me. I felt a distinct message in the core of my being. The Holy Spirit convicted me of my independence. "I don't want you parenting standing up; I want you parenting kneeling down." The scales fell from my eyes as I realized the pride with which I had parented. That was when Psalm 127:1 gained new meaning: "Unless the LORD builds the house, those who build it labor in vain." I am convinced that God designed my son's trials to humble me. If he had transformed Nathan's life as he had Emma's, I would have become the most self-righteous pastor ever, attributing their success to the work of my hands. God wanted the credit for saving my children; I was looking to keep it for myself.

A decade or more before we met, Lois prayed for my salvation in her regular petitions to God for her future husband. Saved at a young age, she understood her need for God and his help in the building of her home. I am certain that when I get to heaven, God will reveal that my salvation was an answer to her prayers.

Having heard that her mother prayed for me long before I was a believer, our daughter Emma set out to pray for her future husband. She started a prayer journal in her later teen years. She prayed that whole first week that God would save her husband. She wrote, "Dear Lord, please keep my husband safe tonight, please watch over him and let him know you are near. God, please pour out your power on him when he feels weak and draw him near to you. Please make him into a man who loves you more than anything the world has to offer. God, when he is feeling tempted, please make yourself and your promises so very real and relevant to him. Lord, you know who this man is and you see all that I can't see, so I entrust him to your care. Thank you for all you are doing and will do in this man's life. I love you, in Jesus's name. Amen."

It wouldn't be until after she got engaged that she would see just how faithfully God answered her prayers, but that is a real-life story for another chapter.

CHAPTER 5

God's Word
Is Able to Save

2 Timothy 1:5 and 3:14-17

Introduction to the Week

Mariano Rivera is widely believed to be baseball's greatest closing pitcher. He had Philippians 4:13 inscribed on his glove: "I can do all things through Christ who strengthens me." In today's baseball, a closing pitcher comes into the last inning of the game, when his team is ahead, to "save" the game. In the seventies, teams called their best relief pitchers "firemen" and brought them in to "put out the fire" when an opposing team loaded the bases, threatening to take the lead. The term "closer" replaced "fireman" when Yankee manager Tony La Russa started using his ace reliever Dennis Eckersley exclusively in the last inning of the game. Like Mariano Rivera, Eckersley was unhittable.

Occasionally, when the opposition loaded the bases in the eighth inning of a game, the Yankee manager brought in Rivera early to save it. Mariano Rivera could shut a team down and save the game with less than a dozen pitches. Nervous fans instantly gained hope whenever he came in the game and thought, *We're going to win this thing.*

Raising kids can be compared to a baseball game. Starting pitchers usually keep you in the game, but it is those later middle innings where trouble can brew. You get a few runs and feel as though you have the game in hand. But make a few mistakes, and you find your family on the ropes in the teen years with the game on the line. In baseball, you bring in your closer, but what do you do in a family, when things go wrong? You call upon Jesus in prayer and you lean on the Word of God. Rivera once shared this insight regarding his own prayers: "People always pray for something they want. He's going to give you what you need."[1]

When your child rebels against you and you feel hopeless, you might be tempted to think that Scripture won't work. It feels dead to you. But the Word of God is living, active, and able to save. The Scriptures can save your floundering faith, and can be used by the Spirit to spark saving faith in your son or daughter. In short, the Bible is the best closer you could have. The Spirit of God, working through the Word of God, infuses fresh faith into the parenting experience, leading parents to believe that "we're going to win this thing."

Day One

An Important Reminder

> But as for you, continue in what you have learned
> and have firmly believed, knowing from whom
> you learned it and how from childhood you have
> been acquainted with the sacred writings, which are
> able to make you wise for salvation through faith in
> Christ Jesus. All Scripture is breathed out by God

---

1. http://christiansportsjournal.com/devotional-mariano-rivera-finds-solace-true-purpose-in-new-testament-verse/

and profitable for teaching, for reproof, for correction, and for training in righteousness, that the man
of God may be complete, equipped for every good
work. (2 Timothy 3:14–17)

Ponder Anew

By the time Paul wrote his letters to Timothy, his once-
young disciple was a well-seasoned missionary with more
than fifteen years' experience traveling from church to church.
The letters reveal Paul's affection for Timothy and are full of
encouraging words and instruction. What is surprising about
Paul's letters is the rudimentary nature of his exhortations.
Having partnered with Timothy in ministry for decades, you
might expect the letter to contain deep theological discourse
explaining the nature of the third heavens or the paradox
between man's responsibility and God's sovereignty. Instead,
we see Paul reviewing the fundamental truths of the gospel,
reminding Timothy of the importance of drawing near to
Christ.

Paul tells his coworker to "continue in what he has learned
and firmly believed," knowing the "sacred writings are able
to make you wise for salvation through faith in Christ Jesus."
Timothy knew Paul's story—that he had been a persecutor of
the church, radically transformed by his encounter with Christ
on the road to Damascus. Timothy was saved through the
preaching of the gospel, so all this is repeat instruction. Still,
in his last days on earth, Paul didn't want Timothy to forget
the key role the gospel plays in their mission (and ours) to see
men and women saved and brought into the kingdom. Aware
that the Lord would soon bring him home, Paul could rest,
knowing that Timothy and others like Titus and Epaphroditus
would continue sharing the gospel, the message that is powerful to save.

Scripture, Paul instructed Timothy, is "breathed out by God." Our confidence that Scripture can transform a person's life comes from this key fact—it is God's Word. Therefore, we can trust that it will work upon the hardest of hearts. The prophet Isaiah tells us that God's Word spoken will achieve the purpose for which God intends and will not come back empty (Isaiah 55:10–11).

As parents, we need to be reminded of the gospel's power to save, especially when our children reject the message we share with them. It can feel like the message isn't working. We think, *Perhaps it works for others, but not for me.* That is the discouragement Paul intended to prevent with his exhortation to Timothy.

First, we must apply the word to our own lives: "that the man of God [or parent] may be complete, equipped for every good work." When we are in the midst of a parenting trial, God's Word supplies us with everything we need to maintain our faith in God, our confidence in the gospel, and our certainty that God's Word is effective and that God will use it to save. Then, in love, we can ask God for ways to encourage our struggling children with it as well.

If, after nearly two decades of ministry, Timothy needed reminding that God's Word is powerful to equip him for ministry challenges, we shouldn't be surprised that we need the same encouragement.

Bring It Home

- When have you been tempted to doubt the power of God's Word to save? Is there someone you've shared the gospel message with that you've given up on, thinking it doesn't work for them?
- How does Paul's encouragement to Timothy apply to us as parents?

Day Two

Don't Forget the Fundamentals

> The saying is trustworthy and deserving of full accep-
> tance, that Christ Jesus came into the world to save
> sinners, of whom I am the foremost. But I received
> mercy for this reason, that in me, as the foremost,
> Jesus Christ might display his perfect patience as
> an example to those who were to believe in him for
> eternal life. To the King of the ages, immortal, invis-
> ible, the only God, be honor and glory forever and
> ever. Amen. (1 Timothy 1:15–17)

Ponder Anew

Do you ever wonder why professional athletes need
coaches? There is a simple reason: even the greatest of athletes
tend to forget the fundamentals. Hitters forget to keep a level
swing and drop their shoulders. Wide receivers in football
forget to look up for the ball, and gymnasts complete a complicated tumbling run but lose track of where they are and step
out of bounds. We all need to be reminded of the basics.

So, even though Timothy understood the gospel, Paul uses
his letters to remind him of the fundamentals of his faith. He
wanted to remind Timothy that Jesus came into the world to
save sinners, including himself, a persecutor of the church. If
Jesus could transform Paul, he could save anyone. Anytime
we struggle to believe that God can reach one of our kids, we
should remember that God saved Paul and transformed him
from a persecutor of the church to a preacher of the gospel. If
Jesus Christ displayed perfect patience in saving Paul, Paul tells
us that we can have confidence in the gospel to save others,
even our most rebellious children.

So, as the Spirit of God leads us, let us share this beautiful message of hope with our children. Our attempts may appear to fall flat, but let us not lose hope. Countless men and women who rejected the gospel early in life then faced severe trials and turned back to the message they first heard from their parents. The seed of the gospel can lie dormant in the soil of the heart. Then, at just the right time, God can command the seed to burst open and grow. Paul on the road to Damascus was transformed by the power of God in a moment. Let us trust God for similar conversions in our families.

Sharing the gospel need not be formal or forced. We need only to depend on the Lord in our own trials and daily challenges and then share the reason for our hope with our kids. Take time to read through a book of the Bible as a family, and the gospel will automatically come through. You don't need to make up the words; they are written down for you! Good preachers know that if they preach through the Bible, their people will get what they need at the proper time. So, if we read through the Bible with our children, a little each day, the gospel message will come through again and again.

Bring It Home

- How can Paul's testimony build our faith for what God can do in the lives of our most rebellious children?
- How prone are you to forget the importance of the gospel fundamentals, like sharing the gospel with your children and praying that God would use his words to transform their lives?
- Do you ever feel like you are not good at sharing the gospel? Does it depend on our presentation or God's power?

Day Three

A Shout-Out to Mom and Grandma

> I thank God whom I serve, as did my ancestors, with a clear conscience, as I remember you constantly in my prayers night and day. As I remember your tears, I long to see you, that I may be filled with joy. I am reminded of your sincere faith, a faith that dwelt first in your grandmother Lois and your mother Eunice and now, I am sure, dwells in you as well. For this reason I remind you to fan into flame the gift of God, which is in you through the laying on of my hands, for God gave us a spirit not of fear but of power and love and self-control.
>
> Therefore do not be ashamed of the testimony about our Lord, nor of me his prisoner, but share in suffering for the gospel by the power of God, who saved us and called us to a holy calling, not because of our works but because of his own purpose and grace, which he gave us in Christ Jesus before the ages began. (2 Timothy 1:3–9)

Ponder Anew

In 2 Timothy 3:15, Paul said that Timothy had been taught the gospel from infancy. In our passage today, Paul gives the credit to Eunice, Timothy's mother, and Lois, Timothy's grandmother.

What did they do? Two things: they believed the Scriptures themselves, and they shared the "sacred writings" with Timothy from an early age. For that, their names were written down in Scripture, recorded for all time for everyone to see. Notice that it doesn't say they saved Timothy. They simply introduced him to the fundamentals of the faith through the Word of God, and the Lord did the rest.

Scripture doesn't give us a ton of details about these women. So, before we jump to the conclusion that they were supermoms, remember that they are included in Scripture for our encouragement. Life was challenging for Eunice: she didn't have the help of her husband, who was likely a Greek unbeliever (Acts 16:1). Lois was likely a widow who lived with her daughter. These two faithful women struggled against sin like we all do; they got angry, lost their patience, and probably doubted God's power to save their children from time to time, just like we do. The key to their success was their faithful devotion to God and teaching his Word to their children. That is something every mother or grandmother can do.

Paul reminded Timothy that it is not our effort that transforms lives, but God's grace. Paul said, "by the power of God, who saved us and called us to a holy calling, not because of our works but because of his own purpose and grace." That is where we, as parents, must find our hope and confidence.

This means that none of our children are too far gone to be saved. Their salvation does not depend on our perfect example or polished gospel presentations. Our children's salvation depends on God's grace, and their rebellion cannot stand against his purpose to save.

So share the gospel once again, believing that God can use it to reach your children. Stir the embers of your faith into flame. Trust that God can save your son or daughter and expect that you'll see them when you get to heaven. When the Lord shares the story of all that he used to draw them to himself, your name will be included.

Bring It Home

- Are you ever tempted to think that your life example is not good enough or that the quality of your gospel presentation is insufficient? How does 2 Timothy 1:9 speak to that faulty thinking?
- What most encourages you from Paul's exhortation to Timothy in today's passage? How can you apply this Scripture to your own life?

Real Life

Lois and Eunice had no way of knowing how their faithful discipleship of young Timothy would impact his gospel ministry. He would grow up to serve alongside the apostle Paul, helping him care for the churches Paul began. Never underestimate the impact of the Scriptures upon a child, even when one parent is an unbeliever!

In the biography that D. A. Carson wrote about his father, he tells a similar story. His grandmother Ethel "was a faithful Christian woman who ensured her children were exposed to the gospel through the ministry of Calvary Baptist Church,"[2] even though his grandfather remained an unbeliever until a few months before he died.

As a result, Ethel's son Tom gave his life to Christ in his high school years and went on to become a pastor. Along with his wife, Marg, he faithfully carried on the gospel mission with their own children, including young Don (D. A.) Carson. Don grew up to become a pastor and seminary professor to whom we are indebted for more than fifty books.

In a message given in his sixties, D. A. Carson reflected back on the influence of his parents:

---

2. D. A. Carson, *Memoirs of an Ordinary Pastor* (Wheaton, IL: Crossway Books, 2008), 27.

I learned to pray by listening to my parents pray. Family devotions and reading the Bible was all a part of growing up. In our family, when we had family devotions, it was our habit for each person to read a verse. Mom always started, all the rest of us read around, it didn't matter how long or short the verse was or how many names it had in it. Just because you were two, and couldn't read yet, didn't mean you didn't participate. No, somebody gave you the next few words, and you would repeat them, and the next few words, and you repeated them. From as early as I can remember.

My father was a pastor. I can remember him preaching Sunday after Sunday to vast crowds of twenty-five. The routine on Sunday was pretty clear. After everyone had gone, he'd play the piano, and we'd sing . . . while the dinner was being made. But every once in a while, dad wouldn't be there at the piano. I'd go looking for him. And more than once I found him on his knees, in tears, in front of his chair, in his study, interceding with God for the people to whom he had just preached, all twenty-five of them. Nobody taught me to do that, except by the modeling, which is everything.[3]

There were also challenges in the Carson home. In an article he wrote entitled "A Personal Testimony of Grace: Growing up a 'PK,'" D. A. Carson was quick to admit that life for his family, like every family, had its challenges.

---

3. D. A. Carson, Transcribed from the message, "The Pastor as Son of an Earthly Father" (Desiring God 2008 Conference for Pastors), http://www.desiringgod.org/messages/the-pastor-as-son-of-an-earthly-father.

When we were growing up, we faced many of the problems confronted by other "PKs" and "MKs." My father was out most evenings: we saw far too little of him, and my mother bore too much of the burden. The family quiet time was not always brilliant and scintillating; indeed, during particularly stressful periods of our lives it could disappear for days at a time. In addition to moral and spiritual pressures, as a family we faced dramatic illness, and at some points financial strain which by today's standards would be considered remarkable: we weren't even close to attaining the heralded "poverty line."[4]

Don's brother Jim rebelled in his teen years, but could not run away from the image of his father praying. Jim recalled, "While walking away from God, I could not get away from the image of my father on his knees, praying for me. It is one of the things that eventually brought me back."[5]

Placing credit where it rightly belongs, D. A. Carson concludes, "Looking back on certain crucial turning points in the family's life, a thoughtful historian would have to conclude that apart from the grace of God all three of us children could have turned out quite another way."[6]

It is important to remember that the fruit of D. A. Carson's labors—the books so many have come to love—can be traced back to the seeds planted in his father's heart through his grandmother Ethel's faithfulness, in spite of the difficulties she faced. Mothers and grandmothers are often the secret weapons God uses to ensure his gospel witness goes forward.

---

4. D. A. Carson, "Growing Up a 'PK'" (*Evangel* 2, no. 4, 1984):16–18. See also http://s3.amazonaws.com/tgc-documents/carson/1984_growing_up_a_PK.pdf.

5. Carson, *Memoirs of an Ordinary Pastor*, 72.

6. Carson, "Growing Up a 'PK,'" 16–18.

CHAPTER 6

New Mercies Every Morning

Lamentations 3:16-27

Introduction to the Week

Sleep is a gift from God that strengthens us physically for the start of a new day. As Solomon said in Psalm 127, "He gives his beloved sleep." The medical benefits of a good night's sleep are well-documented. Sleep allows your body to repair your cells, blood vessels, and muscle tissue. Not only do you rest while you sleep, but your body remains hard at work healing injuries. Sleep reduces the level of inflammatory proteins linked to stroke, heart disease, and diabetes. Sleep helps lower blood glucose levels and improves your short-term memory and long-term recall. Sleep controls your appetite by regulating hormones that stimulate your appetite so that you don't overeat.

A good night's sleep improves judgment, mental wellness, and your immune system's ability to fight disease. A well-rested person is apt to speak and think more clearly and be less irritable, thus avoiding the stress that conflict brings. Sleep helps control pain, helps you drive without accidents, and makes you an all-around healthier person, ready to handle the challenges of each new day.

But something even more wonderful than a good night's sleep comes in the morning: new mercies from God to begin another day. While we should not underestimate the physiological benefits of sleep, our real hope for each new day comes from the fresh portion of grace and mercy that comes down from heaven to sustain us.

Our God is a saving God, and each new day provides another opportunity for him to work his sustaining grace amid our present trials. Yesterday with its troubles is gone, and today, a new day, offers fresh hope. For while we were sleeping, God was at work, for he neither slumbers or sleeps.

The often-quoted biblical phrase, "his mercies never come to an end," shows up in the middle of one of the most tragic stories of all time, the fall of Jerusalem. Countless mothers had watched their sons slaughtered or carried away. If, in the midst of that horrible destruction, God's mercies could be new every morning, then they must be new for us each morning as well. This week we'll learn that we too, who walk through serious parenting struggles, can find new mercies each morning to give us hope, strength, and faith to continue for another day.

Day One

When All Hope Is Gone

> He has made my teeth grind on gravel,
>   and made me cower in ashes;
> my soul is bereft of peace;
>   I have forgotten what happiness is;
> so I say, "My endurance has perished;
>   so has my hope from the LORD."
> (Lamentations 3:16–17)

Ponder Anew

There was no more devastating tragedy than the siege and destruction of Israel at the hand of Nebuchadnezzar's army. The once glorious temple that Solomon had built, which God filled with his glory, lay in ruins, and the survivors were led as captives back to Babylon. God spared the prophet Jeremiah, who for forty years had warned of the coming judgment. He is believed to be the author of the sorrowful reflections we know as Lamentations.

The book of Lamentations is a poetic reflection on the horrors Jeremiah witnessed during the attack on Jerusalem. The walls, gates, and strongholds of the city were broken down and its treasures carried away. The priests and prophets were killed, along with many of the men. Descriptions of horror and violence fill the first two chapters of the book.

Jeremiah himself was bound in chains for deportation to Babylon (Jeremiah 40:1), but he was later released by his captors and given his freedom. The first chapter of Lamentations recounts the destruction, and chapter 2 makes it clear that the Lord brought the terrible judgment upon Israel because of their rebellion against him.

Here, in the verses we read from chapter 3, Jeremiah is bereft of hope and ready to give up. Still, he shares his honest reflections in prayer to God. Jeremiah tried so hard to warn Israel, but they did not listen.

As parents, we can often see how our children's poor choices will end. We warn them of the dangers of drugs, foolish companions, and promiscuity. But they don't always listen. Many of us have been down the same destructive paths ourselves and know first-hand the high cost of disregarding God's law. We so desire for our children to be spared the destruction that we have seen or experienced. In those moments when they do not listen, it is easy to become discouraged. When our children refuse to embrace our counsel and then experience the bad fruit of their folly, it is good for us to grieve before the Lord and honestly share our struggle in prayer. In turning to the Lord we can find renewed hope as Jeremiah did.

It is a great comfort to read through a book like Lamentations or a psalm of lament to see the writers of Scripture present to God an honest reflection of the difficulties they faced. When we see their honesty, we more readily receive their encouragements. Like David in Psalm 3, when he described God as a "lifter of my head," you can call out to God and share your struggles. God will minister to your soul.

Bring It Home

- Take time to pray through a psalm of lament (Psalms 3, 4, 5, 13, 17, 25, 27) and ask God to meet you through the words you pray.
- Write your own prayer of lament to the Lord and trust God to hear you as you use it to call out to him for deliverance.

Day Two

New Mercies Every Morning

> Remember my affliction and my wanderings,
>   the wormwood and the gall!
> My soul continually remembers it
>   and is bowed down within me.
> But this I call to mind,
>   and therefore I have hope:
>
> The steadfast love of the LORD never ceases;
>   his mercies never come to an end;

they are new every morning;
  great is your faithfulness.
"The LORD is my portion," says my soul,
  "therefore I will hope in him."
  (Lamentations 3:19–24)

Ponder Anew

Congregations across the United States sing the modern-day hymn, "The Steadfast Love of the Lord Never Ceases," whose words and title are taken directly from Lamentations 3:22. As they sing, "His mercies never come to an end; they are new every morning, new every morning," many people don't realize the devastating context that surrounded these encouraging words. Yet to know the context bestows upon them a greater power to uplift the soul.

In the midst of Jeremiah's sorrow, with devastation all around him, he called to mind these hope-filled words. Jerusalem, besieged for years, with all food supplies cut off, left everyone desperate for food. The starvation got so bad that the people resorted to cannibalism (Lamentations 2:20). Then the walls of the city were breached, and with that came the slaughter and pillaging of Jerusalem and the desecration of the temple. Mothers watched their children perish and saw those who remained taken into captivity by the armies of Nebuchadnezzar. This devastation left the survivors with little hope that their city could ever be restored.

It is in this context that Jeremiah finds hope in the words so many of us sing. If Jeremiah, walking through the grief-saturated rubble of the once-great Jerusalem, can find hope in God's faithfulness, then we as parents, no matter how challenging our situation, can find the same hope.

Each day when you awake, call out the words of Jeremiah's hope. Shout them aloud for God to hear. "Your steadfast love never comes to an end. Your mercies, O God, are new every morning. Great is your faithfulness."

Bring It Home

- How does knowing that the familiar phrase, "God's mercies are new every morning," was spoken in the midst of great tragedy give it greater meaning for your trials?
- Take time to pray through one of the psalms of lament that speak of God's mercy, faithfulness, and steadfast love (Psalms 42, 57, 77, 86, 89). Ask God to meet you through the words you pray.

Day Three

The Salvation of the Lord Has Come

The Lord is good to those who wait for him,
    to the soul who seeks him.
It is good that one should wait quietly
    for the salvation of the Lord.
(Lamentations 3:25–26)

Ponder Anew

Jeremiah knew ahead of time of the horrible devastation God would bring. He wrote it down on a scroll to be read to the people of Israel to warn them, so that they might repent (Jeremiah 36:1–2). But when the scroll was brought and read to King Jehoiakim, the king cut it into pieces as it was read, and burned each piece in a fire pot (Jeremiah 36:23). His rebellious refusal to repent sealed the prophesied devastation of Jerusalem.

But Jeremiah also knew that the Lord had a plan of salvation, and in that Jeremiah found his comfort. While the sin of God's people was great, God revealed to Jeremiah that his salvation was even greater and would overcome their sin. Consider these prophetic words, which point to the coming of Christ and the salvation God would bring through his Son Jesus.

> "Behold, the days are coming, declares the LORD, when I will make a new covenant with the house of Israel and the house of Judah, not like the covenant that I made with their fathers on the day when I took them by the hand to bring them out of the land of Egypt, my covenant that they broke, though I was their husband, declares the LORD. For this is the covenant that I will make with the house of Israel after those days, declares the LORD: I will put my law within them, and I will write it on their hearts. And I will be their God, and they shall be my people. And no longer shall each one teach his neighbor and each his brother, saying, 'Know the LORD,' for they shall all know me, from the least of them to the greatest, declares the LORD. For I will forgive their iniquity, and I will remember their sin no more." (Jeremiah 31:31–34)

Just as the sins of Israel were horrible and the devastation the Babylonians brought upon Israel terrible, Jeremiah saw a salvation that was even more remarkable. One day God would write his law upon the hearts of his children, and they would all know the Lord, and he would forgive their sins and remember them no more.

Today, we live in the age of this new covenant. Our children are lawbreakers and guilty before God. They grow up, some of them to walk in the same rebellion Israel displayed, refusing to bow their knee. Some of our children have seen the destruction of sexual sins and substance abuse, which have left them devastated like a ransacked city, its walls turned to rubble, and its gates torn down. It is difficult to believe that God will ever save their souls. But remember that we are in the age of the new covenant. God is transforming lives every day. One minute a man or woman is mocking God and the next they are bowing their knee before him, having been born again and transformed by the saving work of Jesus on the cross.

If Jeremiah could wait patiently for the salvation of the Lord as he walked among the ruins of Jerusalem, then we also, with a certain hope for the transforming work of the Spirit of God, can also wait patiently for the salvation of our children. Do not despair, Mom. Do not give up hope, Dad. The salvation of the Lord that God promised has come.

Bring It Home

- Read Lamentations 3:25–26 and allow it to bolster your faith as you wait for God's salvation for your children.
- Take time to pray through one of these psalms of lament (Psalms 31, 41, 61, 64, 141, 142) and ask God to meet you through the words you pray.

Real Life

Maria and her husband, Gabe, poured their lives into parenting their three sons, Destin, Gabe, and Caleb. Gabe Sr. worked hard at his Pennsylvania cleaning business (where I met them) six months of the year. Then, for the other six months, they lived in Florida and ministered through a community-wide drama ministry with a cast of sixty to eighty adults and children. Gabe knew that they had a "fleeting window of opportunity" with the boys during their "impressionable years." Going to Florida enabled the Mahaliks to enjoy a degree of quality family time they were unable to experience in Pennsylvania due to the pressures of running a small business. During these winter months, Gabe set aside time to disciple the older two boys, coach their baseball teams, and involve them in the drama productions he and Maria led and performed. Gabe, in a battle against cancer, saw every day as a fresh opportunity to be used of God. He regularly modeled an active commitment to Christ through evangelism and his love for memorizing Scripture. Gabe was a faithful father.

So when he and Maria received a call from the local Christian school and learned that the school had given their son Destin a drug test, they were shocked. They were initially relieved to find out that the urine test came back clear, but weeks later their world began to crumble when they discovered that their son was involved with drugs and had used another student's urine to pass the test. Apparently, while his parents slept, Destin (age fourteen) took his younger brother Gabe, the keys to the car, and what money he could find to go drinking.

That winter marked the beginning of Maria's years of lament. Destin's rebellion grew steadily, much as cancer took hold of his father. Gabe fought his cancer valiantly while he did his best to speak Scripture and warnings to his son, but Gabe didn't win either war. He died less than a year later, in early September, leaving Maria alone to parent their three children. Destin loved his father, and after Gabe died, Destin was devastated. He went wild, drowning himself in alcohol and further drug use.

In the years that followed, Destin barely graduated high school, then experimented with harder drugs and became hopelessly addicted to heroin. He traveled from rehab to jail to halfway houses to the street and back to jail. Maria lost count of the times Destin went to rehab. Each time he hit bottom, she shared the same message, "I would tell him that God is doing this, he wants your heart. He is not going to let you go. He wants to save you." Destin flatly rejected her counsel saying, "I don't want that, Mom."

"At the end of the day when I laid my head on the pillow," Maria remembers, "I was scared and anxious and really had to calm myself down to even be able to sleep. I slept with my wallet, phone, and car keys under my pillow so Destin couldn't take them. I would pray and cry out to God for help." She always remembered the Scripture that God's mercies were new every morning. She said, "I felt fresh and thought there was hope. God would get me through the night, give me peace to be able to sleep, and I would just wake up with hope. Though at times I also had fear, I knew that God was going to get us through."

It wasn't until eight years later, with Destin in prison facing serious jail time, that he finally gave his life to Christ. With a video hearing coming up, Destin was afraid. His counselor said he'd had too many chances, wasted too many rehabs, and needed to stay in prison. After a phone call from his mom, Destin got down on his knees in his cell and called out to Christ to save him. He prayed along with his mom for mercy. The next day, rather than sentence him to prison, the judge miraculously extended mercy to Destin and allowed him to attend a seven-month program with Teen Challenge. At that moment, Destin knew that God was helping him, but days after the program ended seven months later, he continued his struggle with drugs. While God had turned Destin's heart, the addiction yet enslaved him. It would be another three years before Destin's battle with drugs finally came to an end.

Through those long years, Maria never lost hope for her son and never lost sight of the fact that the Lord is good to those who wait for him. His mercies were poured fresh out on Maria each morning. She was convinced that the salvation of the Lord would come. She wrote Destin while he spent time in prison, recovery, and shelters. Here is a sample of the many letters and emails she wrote.

Destin,

"A righteous man who walks in his integrity.
How blessed are his sons after him." Proverbs 20:7

I think of Dad when I read these verses and what a man of integrity he was. Then, I remember how God has spared you from many dangers and destruction. You are blessed, and God has protected you and guarded your life! I can only believe that he has a call on your life and that he is using this time to strengthen your faith. He is going to make a mighty warrior of God from your broken life, just like he did for your dad. Dad's strength came from his utter trust in God. Jesus set him free from his lifestyle of destruction, and he will do the same for you.

When we talked on the phone last night, and you told me about the panic attack, I thought of 1 Peter 5:6–7: "Humble yourselves under God's mighty hand, that he might lift you up in due time. *Cast all your anxiety on him, for he cares for you*" and how God's Word is powerful. (Well, I admit, that's not the first thing I thought—at first, I panicked, too! ☺) When Dad was sick and dying, we meditated on verses to keep our minds strong through the trial. I believe that is what God is calling you to do. Meditate on the Word of God and anxious thoughts will have to leave. I also get barraged with anxiety and God's Word is a comfort.

My prayer for you:
Thank you that you are breaking Destin's will and conforming it to yours. I pray that you would

help him yield to this painful process. I pray that it would yield much lasting fruit, in his life and in the lives of others around him. I pray that you would use him to be a light to the poor and the addict and that he would be a testimony of your mercy and grace. Pour out your Spirit upon him and give him power to endure. Cause much growth in him as he reads your words and meditates on you. I pray for complete deliverance of drugs, alcohol, gambling, nicotine, lust and all manner of evil and that he would be a man of God with a heart after you. Bring healing to his body and soul. Comfort him, hold him and keep him by your sustaining grace. Help him to see the bright future you have for him—a godly wife, a family and spiritual leadership. We look forward to all you will do in this young man's life. In the precious name of Jesus, AMEN!

I love you, Destin Mark!

Mom

Psalm 116:1: "I love the LORD, for he heard my voice; he heard my cry for mercy.
Because he turned his ear to me, I will call on him as long as I live." (NIV)

CHAPTER 7

Prayer,
Our Doorway to Peace
Philippians 4:4–13

Introduction to the Week

In his book *A Praying Life,* Paul Miller shares how he came to appreciate the importance of praying for his struggling children. He writes:

> It took me seventeen years to realize I could not parent on my own. It was not a great spiritual insight, just a realistic observation. If I didn't pray deliberately and reflectively for members of my family by name every morning, they'd kill one another. I was incapable of getting inside their hearts. I was desperate. But even more, I couldn't change my self-confident heart. My prayer journal reflects both my inability to change my kids and my inability to change my self-confidence.
>
> God answered my prayer. As I began to pray regularly for the children, he began to work in their hearts. For example, I began to pray for more humility in my eldest son, John. About six months later he came to me and said, "Dad, I've been thinking a lot about humility lately and my lack of it." I began to

speak less to the kids and more to God. It was actually quite relaxing.[1]

One of the most helpful promises for parents regarding prayer is found in the book of Philippians, and that will be the subject of this week's devotions.

Day One

It Can't Be That Easy

> Rejoice in the Lord always; again I will say, rejoice. Let your reasonableness be known to everyone. The Lord is at hand; do not be anxious about anything, but in everything by prayer and supplication with thanksgiving let your requests be made known to God. And the peace of God, which surpasses all understanding, will guard your hearts and your minds in Christ Jesus. (Philippians 4:4–7)

Ponder Anew

What do we do when we face serious challenges with our children and anxiety threatens to take us down? Then there are the times we are anxious about something we know shouldn't bother us. How do you deal with that knot in your stomach or feeling of pressure that hangs in the middle of your chest?

Anxiety is elusive. A good cry will often cure sadness, and you can talk yourself off the cliff of anger by pulling away from a conflict or taking a walk. Anxiety is different; it often sneaks up when you don't even know it's coming. You can predict that you are going to experience some stage fright before

---

1. Paul Miller, *A Praying Life* (Colorado Springs: Navpress, 2009), 59.

a performance, or the worry that comes as your roller coaster is climbing up that first hill, but when unexpected difficulties hit you, what do you do? Most bizarre of all is the anxiety that is not connected to any particular challenge. It drifts in one morning like a fog to cast its depressing veil over everything and rob you of peace. How do you handle that? The apostle Paul gives the answer in the fourth chapter of Philippians. "Do not be anxious about anything, but in everything by prayer and supplication with thanksgiving let your requests be made known to God."

Yet Philippians 4:6 is the kind of verse that can feel trite when someone shares it with you. You find yourself gripped with anxiety and a friend, wanting to encourage you, says, "Remember Philippians 4:6," and then quotes the verse from memory. You smile back politely and thank them for their concern, but inside you don't think they have a clue as to just how difficult life is for you. It can't be that easy, can it?

It can help if you know the context of the passage your friend so glibly quoted. Knowing Paul's difficult circumstances can help you benefit from his inspired words that God intends to help us during life's most challenging hardships. Paul wrote the book of Philippians from prison; he had endured a long string of trials that led to his incarceration in Rome. The once-respected Pharisee bore the scars of his service to Christ through beatings, lashings, a stoning, and shipwrecks (yes, that is plural). Now a Roman guard watched him around the clock, robbing Paul of privacy. During this challenging situation Paul learned to quell his anxious thoughts through prayer and he passed on the remedy for anxiety found in Philippians 4:6.

If Paul hadn't shared the details of his imprisonment, you wouldn't know it from reading the rest of his letter. Paul prays with joy (Philippians 1:4), he believes his difficult circumstances have served to advance the gospel (1:12), and he even rejoices when others proclaim the true gospel with false motives (1:18). That doesn't sound like a man in shackles.

So take a second look at Philippians 4:6 and the promise the Holy Spirit offers. When anxiety threatens to drown you, cast your cares on the Lord and cry out to God for the peace he promises to give.

Pray and keep praying until the Lord guards your heart and mind with peace. Sometimes that means you pray once a day in the morning and trust God for the day. At other times, you may need to pray again and again and again. In the most severe trials, you might need to pray almost non-stop. Paul's words are the indestructible words of God; we can trust them to comfort our weary souls. Once we turn to God in prayer and entrust the outcome to his sovereign care, we must say "No" to the anxiety that seeks to rule us and rest instead in the peace of Christ.

Bring It Home

- Read through the list of Paul's sufferings in 2 Corinthians 11:25. How does knowing what Paul went through make his call to cast your anxieties on God (Philippians 4:6–7) more compelling?
- How well are you handling the anxieties that stem from your parenting trials? When in the next day could you set aside time to cry out to God and cast your anxieties on him? Add it to your schedule and follow through.

Day Two

Fill Your Mind with Truth

Finally, brothers, whatever is true, whatever is honorable, whatever is just, whatever is pure, whatever is lovely, whatever is commendable, if there is any excellence, if there is anything worthy of praise, think about these things. What you have learned and received and heard and seen in me—practice these things, and the God of peace will be with you. (Philippians 4:8–9)

Ponder Anew

Anxiety and fear in our parenting struggles have a way of discouraging us and filling our minds with unbelief. Paul's prescription is just the opposite: fill your minds with truth, following the teaching from Philippians 4. Consider these verses from earlier portions of his letter:

- And I am sure of this, that he who began a good work in you will bring it to completion at the day of Jesus Christ. (Philippians 1:6)
- I know that through your prayers and the help of the Spirit of Jesus Christ this will turn out for my deliverance. (Philippians 1:19)
- Work out your own salvation with fear and trembling, for it is God who works in you, both to will and to work for his good pleasure. (Philippians 2:12–13)
- Indeed, I count everything as loss because of the surpassing worth of knowing Christ Jesus my Lord. For his sake I have suffered the loss of all things and count them as rubbish, in order that I may gain Christ. (Philippians 3:8)
- One thing I do: forgetting what lies behind and straining forward to what lies ahead, I press on toward the goal for the prize of the upward call of God in Christ Jesus. (Philippians 3:13–14)
- Our citizenship is in heaven, and from it we await a Savior, the Lord Jesus Christ, who will transform our

lowly body to be like his glorious body, by the power that enables him even to subject all things to himself. Therefore, my brothers, whom I love and long for, my joy and crown, stand firm thus in the Lord, my beloved. (Philippians 3:20–4:1)

Filling our hearts and minds with the truth of God's Word helps us stand firm in the midst of the storm. Jesus said it like this: "Everyone then who hears these words of mine and does them will be like a wise man who built his house on the rock. And the rain fell, and the floods came, and the winds blew and beat on that house, but it did not fall, because it had been founded on the rock" (Matthew 7:24–25).

The winds and the waves may threaten to break you apart, but the rock of Christ as your sure foundation will hold you strong. One day the storm of your trial will end, the clouds will part, and the sun will shine. Until that day, don't give in to the temptations that seek to pull you away from the Lord and his people. Don't give in to believing the lies of the Enemy, which work to convince you that no one cares or all is lost. Believe God's Word and trust him, and the "God of peace will be with you."

Bring It Home

- Which of the verses from Philippians listed in today's devotion encouraged you most? Go back and read the whole chapter from which it came.
- What negative thoughts would you need to put off to make room for the pure, lovely, and commendable?
- Have you shared your anxieties with anyone? If not, who might you ask to pray with you and for you?

Day Three

You Can Do All Things Through Christ

> I have learned in whatever situation I am to be content. I know how to be brought low, and I know how to abound. In any and every circumstance, I have learned the secret of facing plenty and hunger, abundance and need. I can do all things through him who strengthens me. (Philippians 4:11–13)

Ponder Anew

It is not uncommon for anxiety to feed off a deep-seated fear that we will lose something important—your job, your spouse, your health, the love of your child, financial stability, an important friendship, or just about anything meaningful. The crazy thing is that most of us agonize more about something that hasn't happened than we would if we had to struggle with the actual loss.

Rather than depend on temporal things that can be lost, Paul anchored his soul in Christ. The merchant in the Parable of the Precious Pearl (Matthew 13:45–46) sold everything he had to buy one precious pearl. Though he had nothing but that pearl, he now had everything he needed and wanted. That pearl, of course, is Jesus and he fills our lives with meaning, joy, and comfort. He can restore anything this curse-filled world can take from us and strengthen us in the midst of any trial.

Anxiety seeks to keep our focus on our troubles, which means we take our eyes off Jesus. Paul learned to keep his eyes fixed upon Christ (Hebrews 12:2) and lifted them to the heavens, away from his earthly troubles. That is where he found the strength and perspective to endure.

Remember the words of Jesus: "Come to me, all who labor and are heavy laden, and I will give you rest. Take my yoke upon you, and learn from me, for I am gentle and lowly in heart, and you will find rest for your souls. For my yoke is easy, and my burden is light" (Matthew 11:28–30). The message Jesus taught is simple: "Come to me and I will give you rest."

One of the deceptions Satan loves to use against us is to convince us that we are the only family or person with struggles. Everyone else is enjoying a perfect, trouble-free life. But that was not the case for Paul, and it is not what we discover in our churches either. Folks all around you are struggling to find faith for their parenting trials. People tend not to advertise their troubles; they do their best to put a smile on their trials. But if we all hide our difficulties, no one receives encouragement. If we open our lives and share, others soon follow, glad for our example. If you share what you are going through in your small group or Bible study and then ask if anyone else has experienced similar challenges, you will see hands go up across the room. Your humility in sharing may be the very invitation somebody with significant challenges needs to help them open up.

Bring It Home

- What is the basis for Paul's contentment in verse 11?
- Call out to the Lord and cast your burdens upon him. Ask him to be your anchor in the storm.
- To whom can you share the challenges you face and ask for prayer?

Real Life

In the midst of my years parenting teens, Paul Miller published his book *A Praying Life*. I read it from cover to cover. Then I followed his suggestion to write up prayer cards to guide my prayer time. I wrote out a card for each of my six children, asking God to move in one or two key areas in each child's life. Most of these issues represented areas where anxiety threatened me; in some cases, the issues forecasted trouble.

My two oldest daughters, who had been close friends all their lives, were drifting apart. When we started homeschooling our twins, Martha, who is twenty months younger, refused to be left behind. She learned to read, listening to my wife teach her older brother and sister. She never looked back. The convenience of homeschooling three children in one class motivated us to continue, and Martha regularly scored higher in tests than her older siblings. Socially, however, we kept her with her own peer group. By the time Emma entered her senior year of high school, she was hanging with the college students, away from the high school crowd, while Martha was enjoying close friendships with the other sixteen-year-olds. The two began going their separate ways, even though they both planned to start college in the fall.

Seeing this, I wrote out a prayer card which said, "Lord, would you help Emma and Martha see that they are drifting apart and draw them back together and strengthen their friendship. Have Emma reach out to Martha and invite her into her group of friends." Each morning that winter, I went downstairs, started our woodstove, and prayed through my prayer cards.

One morning after prayer, as I passed Martha and Emma's bedroom. I overheard Emma start a conversation with Martha. "I feel like we've been drifting apart," she said. "I feel like the Lord wants me to invite you into my group of friends to strengthen our friendship. Would you like to come along when I hang with the other college kids?"

My jaw dropped. It was as though Emma was reading the prayer card I wrote. There was only one conclusion to draw from that experience—God does hear our prayers and will answer them. God answered that prayer to build my faith for the trials that were yet to come.

In reviewing my old prayer cards to write this story, I was amazed at how many of the prayers God answered. For example, I recently reflected on the blessing that none of our children have ever picked up a deer tick in our yard, despite rolling around in the grass and building forts under the forsythia shrubs. We live in the heart of Lyme disease country, where deer ticks abound and many friends have suffered the horrible effects of Lyme disease. Back when my oldest were in their teen years, I became anxious about them getting bit by an infected tick and the illness going undetected. So I wrote out a prayer card asking "that the deer ticks would be destroyed and no one would come down with Lyme disease unnoticed." Today, looking back, I remember that forgotten prayer and am even more convinced that God protected us. God hears our prayers and he is able to answer them. He is our all-powerful God who can speak to the storm and say, "Peace, be still." He can take away our anxiety and give us peace.

CHAPTER 8

God Understands

Isaiah 1:1-20

Introduction to the Week

The best-selling classic by Harper Lee, *To Kill a Mockingbird*, is a story built on the compassionate wisdom Harper learned growing up as a little girl during the Great Depression. The book, which deals with racial injustice, incorporates a famous American Indian proverb, "Do not judge a man until you walk two moons in his moccasins."

> "First of all," he said, "if you can learn a simple trick, Scout, you'll get along a lot better with all kinds of folks. You never really understand a person until you consider things from his point of view—"
>
> "Sir?"
>
> "—until you climb into his skin and walk around in it." Atticus said I had learned many things today, and Miss Caroline had learned several things herself. She had learned not to hand something to a Cunningham, for one thing, but if Walter and I had put ourselves in her shoes we'd have seen it was an honest mistake on her part.[1]

---

1. Harper Lee, *To Kill a Mockingbird* (New York: Grand Central Publishing, Hachette Book Group, 1960), 39–40.

Nothing helps you sympathize with a person going through a trial more than experiencing that same situation yourself. That is why guys should never comment on the pain of childbirth and why a person who has lost a spouse can immediately connect with someone whose husband or wife recently passed away.

When it comes to parenting a difficult child, people who are blessed with compliant children can be quick to judge other parents for the way their children behave—or misbehave. It is commonly assumed that a proper upbringing would have nipped the problem in the bud. These judgments fly with little regard or compassion for the hard work and hours of conversation the parents of the struggling child have normally logged. The resulting rejection of moms and dads in difficult parenting situations can leave them riddled with false guilt and feeling like failures. If the other parents could walk a day or two in their shoes, they would be more compassionate.

Walking a mile in our shoes is exactly what God did when it comes to parenting. As the self-declared parent of Israel, he experienced the frustration of raising rebellious children. He thoroughly understands the difficulty we face. While others may judge harshly, God extends compassion because he's walked a mile in your shoes. This week we will look at Isaiah 1, where God shares his frustration with Israel as a dad with a rebellious son.

Day One

The Ultimate Foster Parent

> The vision of Isaiah the son of Amoz, which he saw concerning Judah and Jerusalem in the days

of Uzziah, Jotham, Ahaz, and Hezekiah, kings of
Judah.

> Hear, O heavens, and give ear, O earth;
> for the LORD has spoken:
> "Children have I reared and brought up,
> but they have rebelled against me.
> The ox knows its owner,
> and the donkey its master's crib,
> but Israel does not know,
> my people do not understand."
>
> Ah, sinful nation,
> a people laden with iniquity,
> offspring of evildoers,
> children who deal corruptly!
> They have forsaken the LORD,
> they have despised the Holy One of Israel,
> they are utterly estranged. (Isaiah 1:1–4)

Ponder Anew

When it comes to having rebellious children, God understands. He can sympathize with us in our struggles, since he has
endured the rebellion of millions over millennia. His compassion for us in our trouble flows from knowing what it is like to
parent sinful children.

It didn't take long after the creation of Adam and Eve for
things to fall apart in the garden. The serpent deceived Eve, and
Adam joined her and rebelled against God. Despite the countless blessings of their garden paradise, the two of them rejected
God and did the one thing he asked them not to do—eat the
forbidden fruit. Sounds like a few teenagers I know! As a result,
God expelled Adam and Eve from the garden, never to return.

But he offered hope, and promised that one day the head of the serpent would be crushed by the seed of the woman.

While the fellowship they once knew in the garden was cut off and humankind spiraled deeper and deeper into sin, God never forgot the people he created. He remained faithful to his promise, which led to the ultimate adoption process.

First, God called Abraham and declared that he would make him into a great people, and that through his offspring God would bless all the nations of the earth. In the days of Moses, the people rejected God for the first of many times, but it was then that God revealed to Moses that he was Israel's Father, a hint that he planned to adopt us into the family of God.

> "Do you thus repay the LORD, you foolish and sense-less people? Is not he your father, who created you, who made you and established you?" (Deuteronomy 32:6)

If anyone could reform these wayward children, God could. But every single one of his efforts ended the same way. Israel rejected his gracious lovingkindness to rebel and go their own way. Time and time again, the Lord disciplined his children and they rebelled against him.

By the time that Isaiah wrote the opening words of his prophecy, the kingdom of Israel was divided, and both Judah and Israel were headlong into idolatry. This, sadly, reflected their history as a people. After God delivered them from Egypt, instead of delighting in him, they complained in the desert, and made a golden calf to replace him. When it was time to enter the Promised Land, they refused and conspired to go back to Egypt. After wandering in the desert for forty years, they entered the Promised Land, but it was not long before they rejected God and demanded a king, and then turned from God altogether to serve the false gods they'd taken from their unbelieving wives. In spite of God's discipline and many warnings, they turned against him to go their own way. Even God in his mighty power, apart from the cross, was unable to lead his sinful children to righteousness. They must be redeemed. Asaph describes their rebellion in Psalm 78.

> They tested God again and again and provoked the Holy One of Israel. They did not remember his power or the day when he redeemed them from the foe, when he performed his signs in Egypt and his marvels in the fields of Zoan. (Psalm 78:41–43)

So when you call out to God in prayer for your rebellious son or daughter, you are lifting up your requests to a God who completely understands. Isn't it comforting to know that God understands?

Bring It Home

- How are the sins of Israel similar to our struggles and those of our children?
- God related to Israel with grace and kindness. How should his mercy encourage us when it comes to our children? Ask God to pour out his mercy upon your kids.

Day Two

Are You Weary?

> "When you come to appear before me,
>   who has required of you
>   this trampling of my courts?
> Bring no more vain offerings;
>   incense is an abomination to me.

New moon and Sabbath and the calling of
convocations—
I cannot endure iniquity and solemn assembly.
Your new moons and your appointed feasts my soul
hates;
they have become a burden to me;
I am weary of bearing them.
When you spread out your hands,
I will hide my eyes from you;
even though you make many prayers,
I will not listen;
your hands are full of blood." (Isaiah 1:12–15)

Ponder Anew

While the people of Israel continued offering sacrifices to
the Lord, they did not delight in God's law or follow it. They
kept the feasts and celebrations, but they also built altars to
false gods on the high places. Speaking through the prophet
Isaiah, God summed it up with these words: "This people draw
near with their mouth and honor me with their lips, while their
hearts are far from me" (Isaiah 29:13).

After pleading, warning, and disciplining his children time
and time again with little change, God described his feelings
with this phrase: "I am weary" (1:14). Of course, we know that
God doesn't have a mind like ours (Isaiah 55:8–9) nor does he
fall into unbelief or sin (1 John 1:5). Still, when it comes to
parenting, God can identify with the difficulties we face trying
to lead sinful, rebellious children to follow and obey. He knows
what it feels like to become weary.

Historically, God delivered Israel out of Egypt through the
parting of the Red Sea. He led them by a pillar of cloud by
day and fire by night. He provided manna and quail to eat
and water in the wilderness to drink. God gave them victory

in the Promised Land; they simply walked around Jericho and shouted and the walls of the city tumbled to the ground. Despite all this, God's children complained, rejected his laws, sacrificed to idols, and grumbled against his leadership. When Isaiah penned his prophecy, the people of Israel were keeping the traditional sacrifices and ceremonies, but their hearts were far from God.

God could have cut them off forever but instead he patiently continued with them, reprimanding them, reaching out in love, and looking forward to the day when he would pour out his Spirit upon all men (Joel 2:28). One day God planned to exchange their stony hearts for a heart of flesh (Ezekiel 11:19), upon which he planned to write his law (Jeremiah 31:33). Nothing less would save his children from their sinful selves.

If God Almighty could not transform his children through laws, regulations, punishments, and discipline, neither can we. Rules are helpful to protect our children, but they can't save them. God's law was never intended to save; it was meant to show us our need—and our children's need—for a Savior. Yet our tendency as parents is to answer our children's disobedience with a new rule or restriction. There is a time to take away a privilege or draw a boundary, but our hope for their change can only be found in God. Our children need God to pour out his Spirit upon them, soften their stony hearts, and write his law upon them. Until that happens, it is important to know that God knows what it feels like to become weary in parenting. He is not judging you for failing to transform your kids. He knows that only a touch from his Spirit can open their blind eyes to believe in Christ.

Asaph describes God's failed discipline in Psalm 78: "When he killed them, they sought him; they repented and sought God earnestly. They remembered that God was their rock, the Most High God their redeemer. But they flattered him with their mouths; they lied to him with their tongues" (Psalm 78:34–36).

Bring It Home

- The people of Israel continued offering God the required sacrifices while their hearts were far from God. Why wasn't that enough?
- Can you think of a time when you became weary in parenting? How can knowing that God described himself as a weary parent comfort and help you through a difficult parenting season?

Day Three

The Cross Is the Only Answer

> "When you spread out your hands,
> I will hide my eyes from you;
> even though you make many prayers,
> I will not listen;
> your hands are full of blood.
> Wash yourselves; make yourselves clean;
> remove the evil of your deeds from before my eyes;
> cease to do evil,
> learn to do good;
> seek justice,
> correct oppression;
> bring justice to the fatherless,
> plead the widow's cause.

> "Come now, let us reason together, says the Lord:
> though your sins are like scarlet,
> they shall be as white as snow . . ." (Isaiah 1:15–18)

Ponder Anew

In Isaiah 1:18 we see God's solution to the sin of his rebellious children; they need God to wash away the stain of their sin. After mentioning his weariness with their sacrifices, God said he would refuse to hear their prayers (v. 15) and lists the conditions for their repentance.

They need to wash, repent of their evil, and start living righteously (vv. 16–17). But even as God lists these clear requirements, he is aware that they are powerless to fulfill them. Israel cannot wash themselves, nor can they remove the stain of their sin by fresh obedience. There is only one way they will be made clean and thus saved from the punishment they deserve, and that is through the cross.

In the middle of his rebuke, God pauses in verse 18 and says, "Look, let's get real and think about this for a moment. While the law demands your obedience and any hope for restoration requires that you be free of sin, there is no way you can do this on your own. You need me to take away your sin" (my paraphrase).

As parents, this should help us. If the cross is the only solution for our all-powerful God in his parenting challenges, then the cross is most certainly our only hope in parenting our children.

The apostle John shared the same truths in his first letter.

This is the message we have heard from him and proclaim to you, that God is light, and in him is no darkness at all. If we say we have fellowship with him while we walk in darkness, we lie and do not practice the truth. But if we walk in the light, as he is in the light, we have fellowship with one another, and the blood of Jesus his Son cleanses us from all sin. If we say we have no sin, we deceive ourselves, and the truth is not in us. If we confess our sins, he is faithful and just to forgive us our sins and to cleanse us from all unrighteousness. (1 John 1:5–9)

Yes, we must emphasize our children's need to obey God's law, but the ultimate answer to their disobedience is not more rules or stricter punishments. Our children need to confess their sins to the one who can cleanse them from all unrighteousness and wash away the stain of their sin. The cleansing work of the Spirit of God not only removes our past sin but also transforms our desires so that we want to follow God and turn from our wicked ways.

When it comes to our children, let us reason together—the demands and punishments of the law may restrain them, but only the washing away of their sin will save them.

Again Asaph shares God's solution in Psalm 78: "Their heart was not steadfast toward him; they were not faithful to his covenant. Yet he, being compassionate, atoned for their iniquity and did not destroy them; he restrained his anger often and did not stir up all his wrath" (Psalm 78:37–38). The only solution was for God to atone for their iniquity by sending his Son Jesus to the cross.

Bring It Home

- How is Isaiah 1:18 a prophetic reference to the gospel answer outlined in 1 John 1:5–9?
- Too often our children hear more about what they need to do to change than they do about the promise that God can change them. When could you share the grace and mercy represented by verse 18 with your son or daughter?

Real Life

If there were ever a parent that you might think could raise a godly son, it's Billy Graham, but even the twentieth century's most beloved evangelist couldn't make his son, William Franklin Graham III, a Christian.

Franklin (that's what his parents decided to call him to distinguish him from his father) was all boy. He grew up a thrill-seeker who loved anything fast, from cars to motorcycles. He describes himself as a rebel in search of a cause. Though he "made a decision for Christ"[2] at age eight, he didn't experience genuine conversion until his early twenties.

As you would expect, Franklin was surrounded by the same love for Christ in private that Billy Graham preached in the pulpit. His father was a man of integrity and he saw it firsthand. Franklin describes his upbringing: "My parents never crammed religion down my throat. They did try to instill in all of us kids the importance of a personal relationship with God. Every evening our family had devotions before we went to bed. Mama or Daddy would read a short passage from the Bible, and then we would each say a sentence prayer. In the morning, after breakfast, Mama or Daddy would lead us in prayer before we left the house for school. It didn't matter who was in the house at the time—our housekeeper, caretaker or guests—it was something everyone did in our home. I can't remember a day when this didn't happen."[3]

Though his father was gone for months at a time, he gave himself to caring for his son when he returned from long crusades. Franklin's mind is full of fond memories of hiking, camping, and going on special trips with his father—even traveling with his dad to meet the President of the United States. Franklin understood the importance of his father's work and

---

2. Franklin Graham, *Rebel with a Cause* (Nashville: Thomas Nelson, 1995), 122.
3. Ibid., 7–8.

never doubted the sincerity of his faith. While his dad traveled, God was kind enough to provide strong Christian role models for Franklin, and he was surrounded by examples of the transformative power of the gospel. Christianity wasn't phony to him; he just decided he wouldn't play by the rules and would live life his way, as a rebel.

He started smoking in grade school and continually lied about it to his parents. He drank, dated unbelievers, drove without a license, evaded the police on a high-speed chase, stayed out as late as he wanted to while listening to rock-and-roll music. Franklin drank beer, got into fights at school, didn't take his studies seriously, barely graduated high school, and was expelled from college. He lived to torment his sisters, his parents, and his teachers and wouldn't let anyone tell him what to do.

He describes his years in boarding school. "I took pride in my individuality and tried to see how far I could stretch rules before getting reprimanded. Many of these infractions were minor, but everything added to my rebellion. Instead of getting my esteem from achieving within the system, I got my thrills and identity from challenging the system. I was following the classic pattern of every rebel."[4]

In spite of Franklin's poor behavior, his mother and father always reached out in love. Their demonstration of God's love often surprised him. His confrontations with his parents never resulted in them becoming bitter. In fact, Franklin thought his parents were cool and described them tenderly: "My parents made it clear what they would accept or reject in my values and behavior. But on the other hand, they never squashed my individuality or demeaned me as a person. They knew much more clearly than I did the pressures I faced being a 'preacher's kid' as well as the oldest son of a 'Christian Legend.' I'm sure God

---

4. Ibid., 41.

gave them wisdom to know that if they pushed me too hard to conform, I might take off running and never come back—not just away from them, but perhaps from God too."[5]

By the time Franklin was twenty, he smoked heavily and drank often. But his sinful life was leaving him empty and unsatisfied. He felt miserable because he knew his life wasn't right with God. He witnessed God answering prayers anytime he involved himself in any part of the ministry that was his father's life.

On his twenty-second birthday, Billy took a walk with his son and gave him a personal evangelistic appeal. God used the same appeal that drove thousands to their knees in football stadiums, now laser-focused on one boy's heart. "Franklin," his father said, "your mother and I sense there's a struggle going on in your life. You're going to have to make a choice either to accept Christ or reject him. You can't continue to play the middle ground. Either you're going to choose to follow and obey him or reject him.

"I want you to know we're proud of you, Franklin. We love you no matter what you do in life and no matter where you go. The door of our home is always open, and you're always welcome. But you're going to have to make a choice."[6]

After being confronted by a friend a few days later and with his father's words still haunting him, Franklin got down on his knees and surrendered his life to Jesus. Franklin describes that moment. "I put my cigarette out and got down on my knees beside my bed. I'm not sure what I prayed, but I know that I poured my heart out to God and confessed my sin. I told him I was sorry and that if he would take the pieces of my life and somehow put them back together, I was his. I wanted to live my life for him from that day forward. I asked him to forgive

---

5. Graham, *Rebel with a Cause*, 53.
6. Ibid., 119–20.

me and cleanse me and I invited him by faith to come into my life. My years of running and rebellion had ended. I got off my knees and went to bed. It was finished. The rebel had found the cause."[7]

There is no doubt that God used the Graham family's daily devotions, the godly example of his parents, the testimony of answered prayer, and the witness of the solid Christian men who befriended him in the years when his father was away. But none of those good things could save Franklin in and of themselves. Those spiritual influences didn't stop Franklin from smoking, drinking, lying, or doing whatever he wanted. But his parents were not trusting in themselves or these good works to save their son. They were trusting in God and had faith to believe God would apprehend their son. That was evidenced by the countless prayers they offered on his behalf. "Franklin didn't have a chance," they wrote in the afterword of his biography. "He had been given to God before his birth, and God has kept his hand on him without letting up all these years."[8]

---

7. Graham, *Rebel with a Cause*, 123.
8. Ibid., 314.

CHAPTER 9

Turning the Hearts of Our Children Is God's Job

1 Corinthians 3:6–7; Luke 1:8–17; Hebrews 8:8–12

Introduction to the Week

Farmers work hard to prepare their soil for planting. They plow through the packed earth, pick out the large rocks, and throw down fertilizer. When the time is right, they plant their seeds. Then they wait. If the rain is insufficient, they irrigate their fields. Then they wait. They keep watch over their fields to keep out the livestock. Then they wait. They can plant and water, but only God can make seeds grow.

Gardeners know that some seeds are harder to germinate than others. It takes the cold of winter to wake apple seeds out of dormancy. Lodgepole pine cones hold their seeds tight until the intense heat of a forest fire opens the cones. Redbud tree seeds must be eaten and digested to wear away their hard seed coat before they will sprout. Nursery workers can mimic the cold with a refrigerator, use a blow torch to burn resin-coated pinecones, and grind away the hard seed coat of redbuds with sandpaper to mimic the trials that help these seeds sprout and grow. But even so, once they've planted the seeds, all they can do is wait, asking God to bring life out of the deadness of the seed. That is something only God can do.

Day One

Only God Can Sprout the Seed

> I planted, Apollos watered, but God gave the growth. So neither he who plants nor he who waters is anything, but only God who gives the growth. (1 Corinthians 3:6–7)

Ponder Anew

The apostle Paul compared evangelism and the conversion of people to the growing of seeds. We can share the gospel, but only God can make that message grow in an unbelieving heart. When it comes to our children, the same is true. We can plant the seed of the gospel into their unbelieving hearts, but no matter how hard we try, only God can cause the gospel to sprout and grow.

While this might seem like a discouraging reality, it is actually a comforting truth. Once we've shared the truth of God's Word with our children, we can rest, knowing that the sprouting of that seed is not our responsibility. We continue to share the gospel message as the Lord provides opportunity, knowing that he can soften their stony hearts and sprout that seed at any time.

While we wait for God to do his work, we should remember that we can institute rules and discipline, but apart from the saving work of God, those rules and discipline won't soften their hearts to believe. Rather than be consumed with forcing them into a Christian mold, we can rest in our role as truth-tellers. We present the truth of God's salvation, and then we commit the work of transforming their hearts to our all-powerful God.

Can you imagine how discouraging it would be if God made us responsible for changing our children's hearts? If he required us to be a sufficiently godly example or to come up with just the right words that could reach them in their rebellion? That's discouraging! But how encouraging is the truth that God retains that responsibility. We can only point our kids, through the gospel, to a God who saves. Our confidence rests in God's plan to use the story of Jesus as our substitute, dying on the cross, as the means to reach them. The apostle Paul spoke of the gospel's power in Romans when he said, "For I am not ashamed of the gospel, for it is the power of God for salvation to everyone who believes" (Romans 1:16). That word "everyone" includes your children.

We plant the seeds of the gospel, but only God can make them grow. Until he does, we keep sharing the truth that Jesus is the only way, "watering" the seed. We watch like a farmer for the first sign of green popping out of the blackness of the soil. When we see initial evidence of true repentance, we rejoice, knowing it is God's work. Until then we continue to water the seed and wait for God do what only he can do. And as we prayerfully wait for God to save them, we must cast off the false guilt that the Enemy lays on us for their lack of change.

Bring It Home

- What is our role in the conversion of our children? What is God's role? How can keeping our roles straight help remove the temptation to condemn ourselves when our children rebel?
- Look up the following verses to help you articulate the gospel message: John 3:16; Romans 10:9–13;

1 Corinthians 15:3–4; 1 Peter 3:18; Titus 3:3–7. If you memorize these verses, you will always be equipped to share the gospel with your children. You will never need to say, "I don't know what to say."

Day Two

The Time Has Come

Now while he [Zechariah] was serving as priest before God when his division was on duty, according to the custom of the priesthood, he was chosen by lot to enter the temple of the Lord and burn incense. And the whole multitude of the people were praying outside at the hour of incense. And there appeared to him an angel of the Lord standing on the right side of the altar of incense. And Zechariah was troubled when he saw him, and fear fell upon him. But the angel said to him, "Do not be afraid, Zechariah, for your prayer has been heard, and your wife Elizabeth will bear you a son, and you shall call his name John. And you will have joy and gladness, and many will rejoice at his birth, for he will be great before the Lord. And he must not drink wine or strong drink, and he will be filled with the Holy Spirit, even from his mother's womb. And he will turn many of the children of Israel to the Lord their God, and he will go before him in the spirit and power of Elijah, to turn the hearts of the fathers to the children, and the disobedient to the wisdom of the just, to make ready for the Lord a people prepared." (Luke 1:8–17)

Ponder Anew

In his address to Zechariah, the angel of the Lord quoted the prophet Malachi, repeating the very last words of the Old Testament:

> "Behold, I will send you Elijah the prophet before the great and awesome day of the LORD comes. And he will turn the hearts of fathers to their children and the hearts of children to their fathers, lest I come and strike the land with a decree of utter destruction." (Malachi 4:5–6)

Four hundred years after Malachi penned these words, God sent John the Baptist to announce the ministry of Jesus in the spirit and power of Elijah, thus fulfilling Malachi's word. John declared, "Behold, the Lamb of God, who takes away the sin of the world!" (John 1:29). Jesus came to restore our relationship with God and restore the relationships of all God's children one to another. It is the power of the cross that turns the hearts of the fathers to their children and the hearts of the children to their parents.

The transformation that comes when God changes a person's life affects their relationships. Consider Paul's words to the Corinthians: "For the love of Christ controls us, because we have concluded this: that one has died for all, therefore all have died; and he died for all, that those who live might no longer live for themselves but for him who for their sake died and was raised" (2 Corinthians 5:14–15). Through the cross, God forgives us and restores our relationship with him. As a result, believers are motivated to forgive one another, and our relationships are restored (Ephesians 4:32).

The gospel is our hope that our children will no longer live for themselves, and it is our children's hope that God will do the same for us. We will extend the same forgiveness to others that God has extended to us. The result is that our hearts turn toward our children and their hearts turn toward us. Sin creates division, while the gospel promotes reconciliation. Sin fosters selfishness; the gospel propagates grace. Sin brings demandingness; the gospel, servanthood.

If there is a lack of reconciliation, grace, and servanthood in your home, there is good news for you in the gospel. The wait for the one who can turn the hearts of the children back to their parents is over. Jesus has come! Let the gospel first work in your heart toward your children, then patiently wait for God to transform their hearts to respond.

Bring It Home

- What most encourages you from today's devotion?
- If a friend asked, "What was your devotion about this morning?" how would you summarize what you learned?
- Ask God to turn your heart toward your children and your children's hearts toward you.

Day Three

Written on the Heart

> For he finds fault with them when he says: "Behold, the days are coming, declares the Lord, when I will establish a new covenant with the house of Israel and with the house of Judah, not like the covenant that I made with their fathers on the day when I took them by the hand to bring them out of the land of Egypt. For they did not continue in my covenant, and so I showed no concern for them, declares the Lord. For this is the covenant that I will make with the house

of Israel after those days, declares the Lord: I will put my laws into their minds, and write them on their hearts, and I will be their God, and they shall be my people. And they shall not teach, each one his neighbor and each one his brother, saying, 'Know the Lord,' for they shall all know me, from the least of them to the greatest. For I will be merciful toward their iniquities, and I will remember their sins no more." (Hebrews 8:8–12)

Ponder Anew

Does this verse sound familiar? We first looked at Jeremiah's prophecy in Week 7 in our study of Lamentations. The writer of Hebrews quotes it here and again in Hebrews 10:16–17.

A covenant is a contract or agreement between two parties, here between God and his people. The old covenant was conditional, based on Israel's obedience to follow God's commands. God gave them a law and commanded them to obey it. "Now therefore, if you will indeed obey my voice and keep my covenant, you shall be my treasured possession among all peoples, for all the earth is mine; and you shall be to me a kingdom of priests and a holy nation" (Exodus 19:5–6). If they disobeyed, God required them to sacrifice an animal. This process of atoning for their sin through animal sacrifice occurred day after day.

The new covenant is very different. Our right standing before God is not based on our ability to obey the law, but on Christ's perfect obedience on our behalf. Yes, we are called to obey the law, but not on our own. We are called to rely on the Holy Spirit and his ability to change our hearts. In the old covenant, God wrote his law on tablets of stone. In the new covenant, God writes his law on our hearts. Animal sacrifices are no longer needed, for Jesus's death on the cross is the one perfect sacrifice for all our sin for all time.

Now, it is important to remember that until God transforms us by his Spirit, we are not able to obey. Until God writes his law upon your children's hearts and converts them, they are not able to say no to sin with any consistency. That explains their poor behavior before they trust in Christ.

Can you ever remember saying things like, "I'm better off speaking to a brick wall," or "My words go in one ear and out the other," or "She comes to church, but only because I make her," or "He says he is a Christian but doesn't show it"? Parents across the world describe the poor behavior of their children this way, often failing to understand that before God converts them, children cannot properly respond. They are blind to the gospel and deaf to the joyful message it brings.

The good news is that it is not up to us to transform them. Consider what God says he will do: "I will put my laws into their minds, and write them on their hearts, and I will be their God, and they shall be my people." Notice that when God puts his law upon a person's mind and heart, they become his people.

So when we pray for our children, let's be sure to ask God to touch their hearts. He can soften their hearts, write his law upon them, and transform them by the power of his Spirit. When that happens, they will begin to embrace our instruction and follow God's law, empowered by the Spirit of God.

Bring It Home

- How have the Scriptures from this week's devotions bolstered your faith? Are there any areas of unbelief you could confess and ask God to remove?
- When you think of all the areas in which your children need to change, do you see that as something they need to do or something God must do in them?

Real Life

A few months after starting Teen Challenge rehab, Destin's life seemed to turn a corner. He, along with ten other men, were getting saturated with good biblical teaching and worship six hours a day, and it was paying off. This focus on God, away from the temptations of the drug scene, worked wonders for him. I met with Destin's mother, Maria, during that time and I remember her saying that she finally had her son back.

While Destin truly believed that Jesus was real and God forgave his sins, he wasn't strong enough to resist the temptations that assaulted him back in the real world. Once out of Teen Challenge, he found it difficult to believe that he could find his joy and satisfaction in living for Jesus alone. Recalling those days, he said, "When I got out of Teen Challenge, I began gambling on sports and playing poker, and that took away my desire for the Word of God. It was only a couple of months before I was back on heroin, and it got way worse than before. Because I had tasted Jesus and knew he was real, the shame was much greater. More drugs were needed take away the feelings of guilt and shame. It was a horrible existence, to know God and continue in sin."

The resulting chaos brought Maria back into my pastoral office. After multiple rehabs, a prison conversion, and the better part of a year in the mountains of Pennsylvania for Destin, there were no easy answers. Maria had exhausted every earthly avenue available to help her son. But God wasn't ready to give up on Destin. He planned to use the very drug underworld that enslaved Destin to free him from his slavery. Destin recounts the story:

> I grew up hearing the gospel of Jesus every day of my life, memorizing Bible verses, homeschooling, going to church, acting in church plays, and spending time

with my family. That was my life. When I turned twelve, my desires changed. I wanted friends, wanted to be liked, and wanted to feel good. Although I was still around church and heard about Jesus all the time, I didn't care about him. I thought that joy was found outside of Jesus and that I was tricked into believing in Jesus so that I wouldn't be a bad kid.

Soon, I found friends that partied. Within days, I was completely enslaved to feeling good and forgetting about my problems. My journey of bondage and slavery began. As the years went by, the drugs got harder, the consequences were steeper, and the pleasure was diminishing to nothing. At nineteen years old, I was completely dependent on heroin and could not stop. Ephesians 2 talks about us being dead in sin, following the course of this world, following Satan, and carrying out the desires of the body and the mind. That was my life: I do what I want when I want, and I don't care what the result is. Jesus said, "Everyone who commits sin is a slave to sin." I was a dead slave.

In July 2014, as a last-ditch effort to get clean after I failed to stay off of drugs following a seven-month Teen Challenge program, I moved to Allentown to try to "start over." I found drugs within a couple of days. A week later, I was going to meet my drug dealer, and he pulled out a .38 handgun, pointed it at my face, and said, "Don't run." The physical craving for heroin combined with the hopelessness in my soul compelled me to try to get away. He fired one shot at me point blank, and it hit me in the spine. There I was, on my back looking at the sky, bleeding to death in a dark back alley. I remember thinking, *I'm about to go meet*

my Creator, and I don't know what I'm going to say.
Instinctively, I started to scream the name of Jesus.
The bullet went through my lung and stomach so I
couldn't breathe, but I just kept gasping, "JESUS,
SAVE ME!!!" Within seconds I heard sirens, and the
EMTs scooped me off the ground into an ambulance. Then it just went black.

Jesus heard my cry, and he saved me. I lived out
the plea of Psalm 116:

> I love the LORD, because he has heard my
> voice and my pleas for mercy. Because he
> inclined his ear to me, therefore I will call
> on him as long as I live. The snares of death
> encompassed me; the pangs of Sheol laid
> hold on me; I suffered distress and anguish.
> Then I called on the name of the LORD: "O
> LORD, I pray, deliver my soul!" Gracious is
> the LORD, and righteous; our God is merciful. The LORD preserves the simple; when
> I was brought low, he saved me. Return,
> O my soul, to your rest; for the LORD has
> dealt bountifully with you. For you have
> delivered my soul from death, my eyes from
> tears, my feet from stumbling; I will walk
> before the LORD in the land of the living.
> (Psalm 116:1–9)

When I awoke, I was completely overcome with the
love of God. Why would he do this for someone like
me, who just kept running from him? It became real
that God loved me, and it was not based on my performance, it was in spite of it. My faith was quickly
put into action as I told the nurses to take me off the
painkillers. I wanted to be free.

In the days and weeks spent recovering on his mother's couch, Destin read the Bible all day long. He memorized the book of James and several psalms. That study completely changed his perspective. God set Destin free from his slavery to chemicals by opening his eyes to glimpse of the deep, deep love of Jesus.

Destin concludes, "Life in Christ is more rewarding and fulfilling than I could have ever imagined, and as I continue to get to know my heavenly Father more day by day, the joy just keeps increasing. God has saved and transformed me, the chief of sinners, and he has the power to rescue and save ANYONE! There is no one on this planet that is too far gone for God to save through the cross of Jesus Christ. Everyone who calls on the name of the Lord will be saved. When you cry to Jesus, he WILL hear you and answer your cry for help!"

No parent would ever write a script for their child's life that included getting shot as the means to deliver them from drugs. Yet when Maria watches Destin share God's Word with others struggling as he once did, she wouldn't turn back the clock to avoid the shooting. She can see how God used those dark moments to transform her son's life. God alone is the one who knows how to weave a person's story into the fabric of his purpose and kingdom. That is why turning the hearts of our children is God's job.

CHAPTER 10

Who Can Stand Against Us?

Romans 8:26-39

Introduction to the Week

The 1988 French film *The Bear* is the story of an orphaned male grizzly cub that is adopted by a larger mature male, weighing over 1,000 pounds. The two bears find themselves in a life-and-death struggle against two hunters who are determined to hunt the larger bruin down. Amid the chaotic conflict, the two are separated. The young cub is spotted by a large cougar eager for an easy meal.

After chasing the cub over rocky terrain and through a river, the mountain lion catches up with the young bear and the two square off face to face. Though the cougar slashes the little bear's face and draws blood, the little cub holds his ground, stands up tall, puts on his meanest bear face and growls with all his might. Surprisingly, the mountain lion retreats. It is not until the camera pulls back that we see the young cub's larger companion standing eight feet tall and roaring along with his younger friend.

The cub, seeing the giant still roaring behind him, lowers his head, as though he's embarrassed for thinking he had anything to do with the cougar's retreat. But the larger grizzly shakes his head approvingly, giving the credit for the victory to the cub. If the larger bear could talk in that moment, I imagine he would say, "Well done, good and faithful cub!"

The scene reminds me of the way God is at work behind the scenes through our parenting trials. We as parents do our best against insurmountable odds to raise our kids. God is the one working all things together for our good. Yet in the end, he gives us the "Well done" for what he accomplished through us. Knowing in advance that he has our back can give us confidence to stand our ground in parenting challenges. One of the most encouraging passages of Scripture in this regard is found in Romans 8.

Day One

God's Got Your Back

> Likewise the Spirit helps us in our weakness. For we do not know what to pray for as we ought, but the Spirit himself intercedes for us with groanings too deep for words. And he who searches hearts knows what is the mind of the Spirit, because the Spirit intercedes for the saints according to the will of God. And we know that for those who love God all things work together for good, for those who are called according to his purpose. For those whom he foreknew he also predestined to be conformed to the image of his Son, in order that he might be the firstborn among many brothers. And those whom he predestined he also called, and those whom he called he also justified, and those whom he justified he also glorified. (Romans 8:26–30)

Ponder Anew

Did you ever find yourself in a parenting situation where you've run out of wisdom and don't know what to do? You've prayed all the prayers you know to pray and all you're left with is internal angst and a sense of futility that springs from your powerlessness. Sometimes we don't even know what to pray for.

Do you pray for your daughter to be accepted by the popular kids at school or welcome their snub as God's way of protecting your daughter from her people-pleasing desires? Should you pray that your son's team make the playoffs or pray that the season ends early to give your family a break from an impossibly full schedule and help your son finish the school year well? Should you pray that your son gets caught by the police for his drug use or pray that he is spared?

Isn't it a comfort to know that when we don't know what to pray for, God is praying for us. The Spirit intercedes on our behalf, praying in accordance with God's will. Imagine that— in our weakness, the Spirit of God is praying for us and God always answers God's prayers. John Piper, sums it up this way: "God the Father hears the prayer of the Spirit. This prayer is *for* you. And is always heard! Always answered. God does not reject the prayers of God."[1]

There are times when you pray for wisdom for what seems an impossible choice. You want God's will but you don't know what that is.

Should you discipline your son or show him mercy? Should you allow your daughter to go on that date or tell her she is too young? Is it time to let your child develop self-discipline to do his own homework or should you continue to press him to finish his assignments before play? Should you check your son's

---

1. John Piper, "The Spirit Helps Us in Our Weakness, Part 1." From a sermon given May 26, 2002. http://www.desiringgod.org/messages/the-spirit-helps-us-in-our-weakness-part-1.

phone, read your daughter's journal, listen in on a conversation you can hear out in the hallway? Should you insist on drug tests or trust your child's word?

In those moments when we are not sure how to lead, we need to remember that God's will is not a narrow path where all is lost if we miss making the right decision. It is just the opposite. God is so powerful that he works all things together for our good no matter what we decide. So discipline your son or show him mercy. Allow your daughter to go on the date or keep her home. Either way, in all these situations, as we thoughtfully try to discern the best choice, God is able to work all things together for your good.

What amazing truths—the Spirit of God is praying for us and God is working our choices for our good. Parents, you can rest! God has your back.

Bring It Home

- Are there any situations where you are not sure how or what to pray? List them and ask the Spirit to hear the groaning of your heart and intercede for you.
- Where do you need faith to believe that God can work all things together for your good? Make a list of those areas and then pray through the list, asking God to work these things together for your good and to give you faith to believe that he can.

Day Two

God Is for Us

What then shall we say to these things? If God is for us, who can be against us? He who did not spare his own Son but gave him up for us all, how will he not also with him graciously give us all things? Who shall bring any charge against God's elect? It is God who justifies. Who is to condemn? Christ Jesus is the one who died—more than that, who was raised—who is at the right hand of God, who indeed is interceding for us. (Romans 8:31–34)

Ponder Anew

Considering the truths that the Spirit of God is praying for us and God is working all things together for our good, Paul then draws this helpful conclusion: "Who can be against us?" To cap off his argument, Paul brings in the gospel: if God was willing to give up his own Son for us, he will graciously give us all things. The gospel silences any thought that God is withholding good from us. For if he was willing to give up his only Son for us (and we know nothing could cost him more), he certainly is willing to give us what we need.

Anticipating the Enemy's next move—to condemn us as parents for our failures and to convince us that we are not worthy of God's generosity—Paul reminds us that we are the chosen elect of God. This is a choice made before the foundations of the earth were laid (Ephesians 1:4), not based upon our works (Ephesians 2:9). There can be no charge leveled against us, for Jesus Christ took our condemnation on the cross and rose again in a victory we share. It is he who is seated at the right hand of God, interceding for us. So when you hear the Enemy whisper, "You were not a good enough parent to participate in these blessings. You are simply reaping what you've sown," stand your ground and shout, "Get behind me, Satan! I am a chosen child of God, whose failures are covered by the blood of Christ. My prayers may be weak and insufficient and my challenges are great. But the Spirit hears my heartfelt cries and intercedes on my behalf. The risen Christ who died to set me free now sits upon the throne, also interceding. And God my Father in heaven hears these prayers, for God cannot say 'no' to himself. He will answer these intercessions, and by his sovereign power, will work all things together for my good."

The writer of Hebrews, addressing this same topic, concludes, "Since then we have a great high priest who has passed through the heavens, Jesus, the Son of God, let us hold fast our confession. For we do not have a high priest who is unable to empathize with our weaknesses, but one who in every respect has been tempted as we are, yet without sin. Let us then with confidence draw near to the throne of grace, that we may receive mercy and find grace to help in time of need" (Hebrews 4:14–16).

Bring It Home

- Why does Paul use the gospel (God giving his Son to die for us) as the logical reason to prove that God the Father will graciously give us all things?
- How can remembering that Jesus was tempted like us build our confidence that he is sympathetic to our challenges?
- What would it look like for you to approach God's throne with confidence? Act on your answer and make your requests known to God.

Day Three

Nothing Can Separate Us from the Love of Christ

Who shall separate us from the love of Christ? Shall tribulation, or distress, or persecution, or famine, or nakedness, or danger, or sword? As it is written, "For your sake we are being killed all the day long; we are regarded as sheep to be slaughtered." No, in all these things we are more than conquerors through him who loved us. For I am sure that neither death nor life, nor angels nor rulers, nor things present nor things to come, nor powers, nor height nor depth, nor anything else in all creation, will be able to separate us from the love of God in Christ Jesus our Lord. (Romans 8:35–39)

Ponder Anew

In light of the truths we've learned this week—that the Spirit of God is praying for us, that God is working all things together for our good, that Jesus is interceding for us, and that God the Father hears those prayers and is willing to generously give us all things—and keeping in mind that we are the chosen, justified children of God, there is only one answer to the question Paul poses: NOTHING can separate us from the love of Christ! And if we have the love of Christ, then we can be confident that "we are more than conquerors through [Christ] who loved us."

To be sure that all our questions about the truths he's presented are settled in our minds, Paul offers a detailed list of what he's certain will not separate us from the love of God in Christ Jesus. The love of Christ and the resulting blessings will not be taken from us by life, death, or any power in heaven or on earth. Our present circumstances will not nullify God's love for us, nor any future troubles. Then Paul adds the final catch-all categories, "Neither height nor depth, nor anything else in all creation," which covers anything you could think of or the Enemy could throw at you. When we raise our shield of faith in our defense, strengthened by these verses, the Enemy's fiery darts of condemnation and discouragement drop harmlessly to the ground.

Do you realize, Mom or Dad, that there is real help for you in Christ? In parenting your son or daughter, you are discharging one of the most important gospel missions of the church—to raise the next generation, called to carry on the promises of God. You are insufficient for this task, but God never intended you to walk this path alone. He is for you. He is praying for you. He is working all things together for your good. Your failures cannot frustrate his plans. Your child's sin isn't too big for him to forgive; no child is beyond his rescue. So renew your faith in a God who is able to save. Come to the throne of grace boldly on behalf of your children, and he will hear your prayers.

Bring It Home

- Are there any areas of your life that you've been convinced separate you from the love of God? That suggest that you don't qualify for his promises? If so, confess your unbelief as sin and make a fresh commitment to believe the truths in Romans 8.
- Read today's Scripture out loud as a prayer to God, lifting your eyes to heaven. Pray these words with the confidence that they are the inerrant Word of God. Then add your prayer for your family and the challenges you face, doing so with the confidence that comes from believing the Scriptures we've covered.

Real Life

At the time of delivery, most parents are expecting their doctor to announce, "It's a boy" or "It's a girl," not "Oh, look at that. There is a little hand deformity." But that is exactly what the doctor said at the delivery of Bill and Ramona's newborn daughter, Becky. By the grace of God and her work as a pediatric occupational therapist, Ramona instinctively knew that her daughter's shortened right forearm and little nubs of fingers would not severely limit her development. She worked with children to help them compensate for such disabilities. Suddenly, her unexpected change in education and career from graphic arts to pediatric occupational therapy seemed designed by God for her good.

Ramona grew up in a Christian home where her mother instilled in her a love for Scripture. Now, as she held her precious daughter in her arms, she reflected on Psalm 139, one of her favorite passages. In the quiet of her spirit she rehearsed the familiar verses: "For you formed my inward parts; you knitted me together in my mother's womb. I praise you, for I am fearfully and wonderfully made. Wonderful are your works; my soul knows it very well" (Psalm 139:13–14). The doctors explained that Ramona's amniotic sac had gotten tangled over Becky's right limb, limiting the development of her right hand. But Ramona knew it wasn't a chance occurrence. Psalm 139 assured her that it was God who knit her daughter in her womb and that God had ordained every one of her daughter's days before one of them came to be. That gave her daughter's handicap a purpose. It was only a matter of time until she discovered how God would use it for good.

Still, Ramona grieved the loss of dreams she'd had for her daughter. She would never be able to teach her the flute, an instrument that required fingers on both hands. Ramona loved arts and crafts, but thought that too would be difficult for her daughter. Bill encouraged her in those difficult moments with Romans 8:28: "And we know that in all things God works for the good of those who love him, who have been called according to his purpose." That verse restored her confidence in the Lord and the certainty that nothing happens out of his control. His purpose for Becky was good.

Pressure from close family members didn't help. "You need to make that look normal," they insisted and encouraged Bill and Ramona to talk to a pediatric surgeon who could put fingers back on her hand. Ramona's training told her that even the most skilled surgeon could never make her hand look normal. She cringed at the prospect of multiple complicated surgeries. Ramona knew it would only remind her daughter of her handicap and further mark her as different.

Instead of surgery, Bill and Ramona were determined to encourage Becky that God had something big and wonderful prepared for her. They were just waiting to discover what that was. As a result, Becky grew up steeped in an environment of faith and love, which God would later use to draw her to himself.

Life wasn't easy for Becky, who was right-hand dominant, making it difficult to use her left, even though it functioned normally. She got teased a bit in school and was often the last person picked for sports teams, but her real trial came as a young teen when she began to ask, "Will anyone want me with my hand?"

Ramona remembers an intense struggle Becky shared with her when she was fourteen. She told her mom that she was calling out in prayer saying, "God, you haven't healed me, even though I've asked more times than I can count. Why did it have to be my right hand? If only you'd have taken my left hand instead. I could meet new people and shake hands without feeling embarrassed. Learning to write would have been so much easier and my handwriting would be so much better." Then she felt the Lord impress a word upon on her soul. "You'll be able to wear your wedding ring on your left hand." That message stopped her complaining. God had preserved the fingers on her left hand so that she would be able to receive a ring from her husband. Becky cherished this and wrote it in her journal.

While Becky never did play the flute, she did take up French horn, and became an honor student with the unique left-handed instrument. She also surprised Ramona with her artistic gifts. Though she was right-hand dominant, she learned to crochet with her left hand and create fine jewelry. She eventually started a business that had sales as far away as Europe.

I first met Becky while I was teaching the grade school Sunday school class. It took me a while to get comfortable and not stare at her right arm. I found myself praying that God would use her handicap to keep her hidden from guys who are concerned with outward appearances and to preserve her for a godly man who would see through her handicap to her godly character.

In time, God brought Justin into her home, a friend of her brother Steve. Justin got to know Becky well as he hung out with Steve and the family, but it wasn't until a pastor recommended he consider her more seriously that the thought of marriage to Becky entered his mind. Justin approached Bill and asked him for permission to pursue Becky. After Bill's conversation with Becky and no small amount of prayer, Bill and Ramona consented and Justin and Becky started their courtship.

Very early on, Justin felt that God gave him an idea for the perfect proposal. The moment came a few months later while he and Becky were enjoying a campfire under a star-filled sky. He pulled out the ring and said, "May I put this ring on your finger?" Becky said yes and Justin then shared that he believed the Lord had preserved the fingers of her left hand to receive the ring, sharing nearly the same impression the Lord had given Becky eight years earlier.

Becky later told her mom, "In that moment it was as if God was saying, 'You really heard me ten years ago. This was all a part of my good plan for you, and here is the man I've been preparing for you!'" Becky later showed Justin the journal entry where she had recorded the encouragement the Lord gave her.

Reflecting on that special day, Ramona recalled, "Not only did we rejoice in the wonderful news of Becky and Justin's engagement, but even more so in the very detailed and specific care of our kind, sovereign, and benevolent Savior, who did not let us miss his 'handiwork' in Becky's life."

CHAPTER 11

He Is with You

Isaiah 41:8-13; John 14:18-23; Revelation 20:1-4

Introduction to the Week

I recently visited the National Gallery of Art in Washington D.C., where a friend introduced me to a series of four paintings entitled "The Voyage of Life," by Thomas Cole. The paintings hang on four opposing walls in thick, gilded frames with doorways between them. The series of paintings depicts our journey from birth to death as a gondola trip on the river of life.

In the first painting, "Childhood," we see an infant boy lying on a bed of flowers in the gondola, full of delight, without a care. The vessel is adorned with a figurehead holding an hourglass to indicate the passing of time. Standing behind the child, an angel steers the boat safely upon a river that originates in the mouth of a cave. In the second painting, "Youth," the child has grown to become a young man. He now steers the vessel, with the angel waving from the shore, ever watchful, but leaving the man to plot his own course.

The third in the series, "Manhood," presents a foreboding scene, where the fully mature man confronts a severe trial, a section of violent rapids and sharp rocks. Evil spirits are visible in the dark storm clouds overhead. But rather than grasping the tiller, the man is portrayed on his knees, with hands folded in prayer. While he feels alone and afraid, we see a window from heaven opened behind him, from which the angel is faithfully looking down, guarding the man.

Finally, in the last painting, "Old Age," the angel once again stands with the man in the boat, to guide him to the safe end of his journey. The waters have calmed, the hourglass that once adorned the prow of his vessel is gone. The aged man is at peace, aware of the presence of the angel for the first time. He is ready to meet his Maker.

As I took in this series of paintings, I wished for the maturity of the older man and the lesson he learned in the rapids: despite the harrowing dangers of life, God is ever watching over us and we can place our trust in him. In our voyage of life, we do not travel alone. That is the testimony of Scripture and the subject of our study this week.

Day One

Fear Not, For I Am with You

> But you, Israel, my servant, Jacob, whom I have chosen, the offspring of Abraham, my friend; you whom I took from the ends of the earth, and called from its farthest corners, saying to you, "You are my servant, I have chosen you and not cast you off"; fear not, for I am with you; be not dismayed, for I am your God; I will strengthen you, I will help you, I will uphold you with my righteous right hand. (Isaiah 41:8–10)

Ponder Anew

These tender, comforting words of Isaiah 41 come after Isaiah prophesied the destruction of Jerusalem and the captivity of God's people by the nation of Babylon (Isaiah 39:6–8). While the people in Isaiah's day mostly rejected the words he spoke, they became a hope-filled comfort for anyone captive in Babylon fortunate enough to hear them. Imagine for a moment that you are one of the young men carried off into Babylon, now reading these words. What a comfort! Now apply those words to your own trial. They are meant to bring encouragement and hope to your heart in just the same way.

While it is important to study the original context of Scripture, it is equally important to apply the Scriptures to our own lives. As God comforted his chosen people of old through their trials, he also means to comfort us. When God assures Israel that he is with them, we can be certain that he is also with us. As Christians, we too are chosen by God. The apostle Peter writes, "You are a chosen race, a royal priesthood, a holy nation, a people for his own possession, that you may proclaim the excellencies of him who called you out of darkness into his marvelous light. Once you were not a people, but now you are God's people; once you had not received mercy, but now you have received mercy" (1 Peter 2:9–10).

So soak in the good of Isaiah's words through your parenting trials. Consider the heart of God as revealed by the prophet for you:

> "Fear not, for I am with you." There is no more comforting word than that God is with us. If he is with us, he sees our trials and knows what to do to help us.
>
> "Be not dismayed, for I am your God." With these words, God reveals his disposition; not only is he with us, he is also for us.

"I will strengthen you." Now come the promises that we who are chosen can take to the bank. When we are weary, God will renew our strength.

"I will help you." This phrase is not a conditional statement. God will help his chosen children through their trials.

"I will uphold you with my righteous right hand." While God does not promise to take all our trials away, he does promise to be with us, to strengthen us, help us, and uphold us; he will ensure that we do not fail. We base our confidence in approaching God on the sacrifice of Jesus, who lived a perfect life and exchanged it for our life of sin.

After delivering Israel through the Red Sea, God's people rebelled and rejected him for a golden calf. In response to their rebellion, God told Moses that he would send an angel to go with them to the Promised Land but he himself would not go, lest he destroy Israel in their sin (Exodus 33:2–3). The people mourned when they heard God's decree. Moses later appealed, saying, "If your presence will not go with me, do not bring us up from here. For how shall it be known that I have found favor in your sight, I and your people? Is it not in your going with us, so that we are distinct, I and your people, from every other people on the face of the earth?" (Exodus 33:15–16). Then came these most comforting words from God in reply. "This very thing that you have spoken I will do, for you have found favor in my sight, and I know you by name" (Exodus 33:17).

Isaiah is simply repeating to Israel what God first promised Moses, that God would go with them despite their sin. God's gifts and calling are irrevocable (Romans 11:29) and he is the same, yesterday, and today, and forever (Hebrews 13:8). So we, God's chosen people, whom he knows and calls by name (John 10:3), can be confident that his presence goes with us too, to strengthen, help, and uphold us through our parenting trials.

Bring It Home

- Imagine that Isaiah is prophesying to you directly through today's passage. Where could you use a little strength and help? Offer these areas in prayer to God, appealing to the promises in Isaiah's prophecy.
- Why do we find it so difficult to believe that God is with us when we go through trials?

Day Two

The Spirit Dwells with Us

> "I will not leave you as orphans; I will come to you. Yet a little while and the world will see me no more, but you will see me. Because I live, you also will live. In that day you will know that I am in my Father, and you in me, and I in you. Whoever has my commandments and keeps them, he it is who loves me. And he who loves me will be loved by my Father, and I will love him and manifest myself to him." Judas (not Iscariot) said to him, "Lord, how is it that you will manifest yourself to us, and not to the world?" Jesus answered him, "If anyone loves me, he will keep my word, and my Father will love him, and we will come to him and make our home with him." (John 14:18–23)

Ponder Anew

With the sending of the Holy Spirit at Pentecost, Jesus delivered on the promise he made to his disciples and fulfilled the Old Testament prophecies that foretold that God would once again live among his people. Imagine living in the time of Moses, seeing the pillar of cloud by day and fire by night, or during Solomon's reign, watching the pillar of fire descend upon the temple, knowing that God dwelt among his people. Still, neither the presence of God in the pillar of cloud and fire or the fire that filled the temple compare with the presence of the Holy Spirit, who dwells in the hearts of every believer individually.

Consider how amazing it is that all Christians have the Holy Spirit living in us! In the years following the exodus, it was very different. Moses was the only one who met with God personally in the tabernacle. Later, with the building of Solomon's temple, only the high priest entered the Holy of Holies to offer sacrifices in God's presence. Today this privilege extends to every believer. Each of us is a temple of the Holy Spirit (1 Corinthians 3:16).

That means that at any point in our day, we can approach God's throne of grace simply by dropping to our knees and speaking out in prayer. Each of us, like Moses slipping through the curtained doorway of the tabernacle, can talk directly with God. Every one of us has access to God, just as the high priest who entered the temple. But we come not with the blood of bulls or goats; we come by way of Jesus's shed blood on the cross. While a pillar of smoke or fire isn't going to descend upon our house, Scripture teaches that the same presence of God, by his Holy Spirit, is with us nonetheless.

Notice how relationally experiential the dwelling of the Spirit is in the life of the believer. "In that day you will know that I am . . . in you" (v. 20). Jesus promises to manifest his presence to us. That is not just a presence we understand intellectually, but one we can experience, feel, and know.

What a comfort that brings as we walk through the trials of life! We are aware that we are not walking alone; God is with us. When we drop to our knees in prayer, he already knows what we need, even before we pray. He is with us in our trials and remains with us through them. Christians who depend on the Spirit of God through their trials often say, "I don't know how unbelievers do it without God!"

The believers who struggle most are those who are unaware of the resource we have in the Holy Spirit. The Spirit convicts us of sin and opens the Scriptures to help us understand God's Word and apply it to our lives. He gives us the gift of faith to trust God for our deliverance and provides us with an internal assurance of his presence. This acts as our guarantee of eternal life and the end to all our suffering.

So hear the promise of Jesus for you and personalize it by adding in your name:

> "I did not leave you as an orphan, Mary, Carlton, Sherri, Edward; I came to you. The world does not see me, but you see me. You know that I am in my Father, and you in me, and I in you. I love you and manifest myself to you and have come to make my home with you."

No parenting trial can take the Spirit of God away from you. Our fellowship with the Holy Spirit provides the comfort we need to stand firm in faith.

Bring It Home

- Where in Jesus's promise do you see the Trinity (Father, Son, and Holy Spirit)?
- Compare the average Christian's experience of the Holy Spirit with the unique experience Moses had or the Spirit filling the temple. How does it help you to appreciate the amazing gift we have in the presence of the Holy Spirit in the life of every believer?

- If you are a Christian, thank God for sending his Spirit to you. If you have not yet placed your trust in Jesus Christ and his sacrifice on the cross for your sin, confess your sin to God and ask him to fill you with his Holy Spirit, that you might know God's presence within you.

Day Three

Dreaming of Heaven

Then I saw a new heaven and a new earth, for the first heaven and the first earth had passed away, and the sea was no more. And I saw the holy city, new Jerusalem, coming down out of heaven from God, prepared as a bride adorned for her husband. And I heard a loud voice from the throne saying, "Behold, the dwelling place of God is with man. He will dwell with them, and they will be his people, and God himself will be with them as their God. He will wipe away every tear from their eyes, and death shall be no more, neither shall there be mourning, nor crying, nor pain anymore, for the former things have passed away." (Revelation 21:1–4)

Ponder Anew

Before experiencing the trials that parenting brought to me, I didn't dream of heaven, nor did I long for the Lord's return. I read passages like Revelation 21 but, quite honestly, I was enjoying life too much to think much about God. I dreamt of finding a lost treasure, catching a trophy fish, or achieving success in some aspect of life. Since life was running smoothly, I could keep God in my box and take him out for Sunday morning and daily devotions. The result was that God didn't factor much into my dreams. But the trials and disappointments of life changed that. God used my trials to help me long for the Lord's return and the scene described in Revelation 21.

When I was around four years old. I remember falling and getting hurt. My mom lifted me into her lap, wiped away my tears, and laid my head on her shoulder while holding me tight. The love and reassurance I felt at that moment were so strong that it burned onto the deepest part of my mind. It is a memory I've recalled in some of life's most difficult moments. Heaven with God is going to be like that. Imagine a day when the Lord returns to draw us near and wipe away our every tear, put an end to all our trials, suffering, diseases, and disappointments, and replace them with everlasting joy, conflict-free relationships, and harmony with everything and everyone. Now add one more word—forever! "Death shall be no more, neither shall there be mourning, nor crying, nor pain ANYMORE!" We will live with our King and Savior Jesus Christ and see him as he is, face to face (1 John 3:2; 1 Corinthians 13:12).

Part of the reason I never dreamt much of heaven is that my conception of heaven was shaped more by Saturday morning cartoons than the Bible. I imagined floating around on clouds with the angels, singing praise songs day and night. But the Bible presents an entirely different view of heaven. God is going to destroy the earth as we know it, re-create it to be brand new, and then come to earth to live with us in a world free of sin, temptation, suffering, and pain. The best part of all is knowing that we will finally be able to fulfill our intended purpose—to glorify God and enjoy him forever.

Looking back at my parenting trials, I see how God used them to help me see a true picture of this sinful, trouble-filled world, filled with empty promises. Against the backdrop of sadness and sorrow, the joys of heaven shine. Today, I long for the Lord's return and can't wait for the Lord to destroy all evil, re-create the earth and restore us to fellowship with him. I long to enjoy the day when I walk with Jesus in my resurrected, sin-free body and look upon his face. And my joy in that moment will last forever and ever!

Bring It Home

- How has God used trials to help you see the empty promises of this earthly life?
- Read through the rest of Revelation 21. Imagine what it will be like when all our trials are over. Now imagine being there with all of your children. While our faith is weak at times to believe that some of them will ever get to heaven, we need to remember that "the arm of the LORD is not too short to save" (Isaiah 59:1 NIV). God is able to rescue the most rebellious of our kids.

Real Life

Christopher and Nancy knew something was seriously wrong when their ultrasound technician quietly left the room to get the doctor. A moment later, the doctor, a genetic specialist, looked at the images and then turned to the Campbells. "I'm very sorry to tell you this, but there is something very wrong with your baby." He went on to explain that the sac of fluid showing at the base of their baby's neck indicated a 98 percent probability of a genetic defect. The doctor pulled out a chart, ran his finger down to the appropriate column, and read the stats. Sixty percent of babies with a similar buildup of fluid don't make it to twenty weeks, seventy-five percent of those who reach twenty weeks are not born alive, and of those who are, ninety-nine don't make it to their first birthday. Without missing a beat, the doctor continued, "We can refer you to someone who can counsel you regarding this genetic information and refer you to someone to help you with next steps." When Christopher and Nancy asked what he meant by "next steps," the doctor said, "I would consider terminating the pregnancy given these initial findings."

Once the diagnosis of Trisomy 18 was confirmed, Christopher and Nancy never heard the word "baby" from their doctors again. They met Christopher and Nancy's refusal to abort with an escalating rhetoric of fear. The physicians they had trusted to deliver their baby turned against them and said that their pregnancy was "incompatible with life," would ruin their marriage and family, and was a "useless, wasted pregnancy." As their pastor, I remember those difficult early days of comforting Christopher and Nancy, astonished at how insensitive Nancy's ob-gyn acted in response to their decision to carry their baby.

The realization that they may never meet their baby hit Christopher and Nancy hard, and they began to grieve. It was so emotionally overwhelming for Nancy that it was difficult for her to pray. Christopher held her while she sobbed and prayed over her. Recalling those difficult moments, Nancy said, "It felt as though God was holding us." Judah, their bright two-and-a-half-year-old son, wanted to know, "Why is Mommy so sad?"

Help finally came to the Campbells through a "random" phone call from Mary, a genetic counselor connected to the lab that processed Nancy's blood work. When Nancy explained that she was not terminating her pregnancy, Mary didn't push back like the other doctors. Instead, she offered to help. Christopher conferenced in from work, and the two of them learned for the first time that they were having a girl. "Have you thought of any names?" the counselor asked. "We are going to call her Nora," Nancy replied. Then Mary offered to refer them to Children's Hospital of Philadelphia (CHOP), the hospital that would take over "Nora's" care.

Soon Christopher and Nancy were receiving expert care by some of the top neonatal specialists in the country. They were accepted by CHOP into their Garbose Family Special Delivery Unit, the world's "first birthing unit within a pediatric hospital dedicated to healthy mothers carrying babies with serious and life-threatening birth defects."[1] From that point on, Nora was never referred to as a fetus again and she had a team of doctors dedicated to her care.

Nancy and Nora received regular ultrasounds at CHOP by a top pediatric fetal geneticist. Their doctor, noticing that Nora's hands were formed with her index fingers pointing out, laughed and started calling her Annie Oakley, saying "She's got her guns out again." The 3D ultrasounds became the way Christopher and Nancy got to know their daughter.

As their delivery date approached and end-of-life decisions were laid out before them, Christopher and Nancy leaned upon the Lord for wisdom like never before. "As an engineer," Christopher said, "I could fix everything in my life, but I realized with Nora, there was nothing I could do to fix this. God taught me how much I really did not trust God and how self-reliant I lived day to day."

Nancy knew that God answered their prayers to allow Nora to survive her birth when, a few minutes into an emergency C-section, Nancy heard Nora cry. The nurses allowed Christopher to hold his daughter while they assessed her. One of the nurses took pictures for the Campbells. As the minutes passed, Nora became more quiet. At the end of the assessment, the neonatologist shook her head as Christopher handed Nora to Nancy and said, "There is nothing we can do." Reflecting on those moments, Christopher said, "We didn't have any decisions to make. God took control of the situation and made it clear that Nora's life was ending soon. She never opened her eyes, but she held my finger."

Nora didn't struggle. She quietly settled on Nancy's chest, breathing slowly as Nancy held her. Nancy recalled Nora's

1. http://www.chop.edu/centers-programs/garbose-family-special-delivery-unit/about

final moments saying, "Her heart rate continued to slow. We watched her quietly go. We told her we loved her, prayed with her, and we both kissed her goodbye."

By this time, I had arrived at the hospital and waited with the grandparents to meet Nora. When my turn came, an hour or so after her birth, she had already passed. I had to agree with everyone's assessment. Nora was beautiful.

As an extension of honoring life, the staff in the Special Delivery Unit understood dignity in death and the importance of giving parents the opportunity to grieve the loss of their child. They allowed the Campbells to keep Nora in Nancy's room. Any time the CHOP staff entered, from the top doctors down to the kitchen staff, they would express their sorrow and ask if they could greet Nora and report to the Campbells how beautiful she was.

The CHOP staff took plaster casts of Nora's feet. They welcomed Nora's brother, Judah, and allowed him to paint with his sister, as they moved her lifeless arms to create a memory for her older brother. They used an ink pad to make prints of Nora's hands and feet. Christopher and Nancy placed her handprint on two verses. Psalm 139 and Revelation 21. Christopher said, "The two verses encapsulated our thoughts, that God knit Nora together in Nancy's womb and one day, God will restore the creation and fix all Nora's problems."

"I think Revelation 21 never seemed so beautiful than in that moment," Christopher shared. "Up until that day, the earth seemed quite comfortable to me. Now the earth seems a lot paler and has lost its shine. Now we long for heaven. All of life's trials are because the world is fundamentally broken. The hope we hold is that one day he will make all things new." Nancy added, "Not just the erasing of our sorrow, but the joy that will come from being reunited with her." Today, when someone asks Judah how many siblings he has, he will say, "I have two. One that is dead, but that is okay, she lives in heaven and is joyful and safe. And I have one who lives on earth."

When it was time to say goodbye to Nora, the day of Nancy's discharge, the staff of the Special Delivery Unit gave the Campbells a memory box filled with her mementos. Every year the Campbells are welcomed back to the hospital around Christmastime, along with all the parents who have lost children at the unit, for a candlelight service and slide-show. Afterwards, the staff creates a yearbook with the photos of the slideshow and letters from the parents to their children. Christopher said, "God never lost sight of Nora, and he sent 'random' people to care for her. God never left our tomorrow to chance."

CHAPTER 12

Not One Will Be Lost

Matthew 18:10-14; Luke 15:3-7, 11-32

Introduction to the Week

It's hard for those unfamiliar with shepherding to identify with the depth of love a shepherd has for his sheep. But if Jesus had told a parable about a lost sheepdog instead, folks would immediately understand the grief of the shepherd searching for his lost dog.

People will go to great lengths to find a lost canine. There is even a non-profit organization dedicated to helping people find their missing pets. It was founded by a former police officer who has helped hundreds of dog owners recover their lost canines with the help of trained bloodhounds. Owners of lost pets are desperate when they call for help and usually thin on hope after days of searching with no success. But when you put good bloodhounds on a trail, even one that is weeks old, they routinely find the lost dogs. And when a lost dog is found, the reunion with their master is a perfect picture of how a shepherd would react to finding his lost sheep. They run to their dog and lavish it with affection.

Better still is to think of a parent with a toddler on a crowded beach. It takes all of about two milliseconds for a restful day to give way to an all-out frenzied search when we realize that our child has wandered off and is lost. At that moment, nothing will stop us from finding them. That is the same fervor with which a shepherd goes after his lost sheep. The image is meant to help us see how intently God goes after his lost sons and daughters. So if you have a wayward child, draw comfort from these devotions and rest in the truth that God is on a mission to seek and save the lost.

Day One

He Leaves the Ninety-Nine

> "See that you do not despise one of these little ones. For I tell you that in heaven their angels always see the face of my Father who is in heaven. What do you think? If a man has a hundred sheep, and one of them has gone astray, does he not leave the ninety-nine on the mountains and go in search of the one that went astray? And if he finds it, truly, I say to you, he rejoices over it more than over the ninety-nine that never went astray. So it is not the will of my Father who is in heaven that one of these little ones should perish." (Matthew 18:10–14)

Ponder Anew

Christian parents should draw comfort from this passage, for it is right and good for us to trust that our children are numbered with the "little ones" Jesus is talking about. Scripture sets the expectation for parents to believe for the salvation of their children. When they go astray, let's call out to Jesus to join the search, for it is the Father's will that every last lost one of his sheep be found and rescued.

The writer of Hebrews tells us that angels are "ministering spirits sent to serve those who will inherit salvation"

(Hebrews 1:14 NIV). Angels ministered to Jesus after his temptation in the wilderness (Matthew 4:11) and again at Gethsemane, when an angel appeared to strengthen Jesus (Luke 22:43). Here Jesus reveals that angels are given assignments to watch over the little ones the Father plans to save. While we don't know angels' exact job description in serving believers on earth, it is a comfort to know that they are on assignment from heaven. And while commentators discourage us from reading into this passage that specific guardian angels are assigned to children individually, we can pray to God with confidence, asking him to send his angels to guard our children when they are apart from our care.

The story of Zacchaeus exemplifies Jesus's searching for a lost sheep. Zacchaeus climbs a tree to get a look at Jesus, the traveling teacher, but it is Jesus who leaves the crowd, walks up to his tree and calls Zacchaeus down. After inviting himself to Zacchaeus's house for dinner, Jesus announced, "Today salvation has come to this house, since he also is a son of Abraham. For the Son of Man came to seek and to save the lost" (Luke 19:9–10).

The good news for us as parents is that God's mission to seek and save the lost did not end with Christ's return to heaven. The Spirit of Christ is still seeking and saving our lost children. So when one of your children goes astray, call out to God to send his angels to watch over him and ask Jesus to seek and save him from his sin.

The Enemy is ever ready to discourage us with unbelief and doubt. He wants you to believe that your child is beyond the reach of the Shepherd, or that your son or daughter is not numbered among the sheep of God, which explains why no rescue attempt has come. But we must cast off Satan's predictable accusations, put our faith and trust in our compassionate Savior, and redouble our efforts to pray. We pray against the attacks and lies of the Enemy, while we cry out to the Father for daily help and for the Good Shepherd, Jesus, to rescue our sons and daughters from their wandering and sin.

Bring It Home

- How should knowing that God will not let a single one of his children perish encourage your faith for your wayward children?
- Take time to ask the Lord to seek out your children, like the lost sheep in the parable.

Day Two

Lost Sheep, Take Two

> So he told them this parable: "What man of you, having a hundred sheep, if he has lost one of them, does not leave the ninety-nine in the open country, and go after the one that is lost, until he finds it? And when he has found it, he lays it on his shoulders, rejoicing. And when he comes home, he calls together his friends and his neighbors, saying to them, 'Rejoice with me, for I have found my sheep that was lost.' Just so, I tell you, there will be more joy in heaven over one sinner who repents than over ninety-nine righteous persons who need no repentance." (Luke 15:4–7)

Ponder Anew

Repetition in the Scriptures is not accidental; it can help us draw additional insights. Some of the details in Luke's account of the parable are different from Matthew's version, which we just read. Jesus likely spoke the same parables to multiple audiences and didn't always keep the details the same.

In Luke's version of the parable of the lost sheep, the shepherd is so intent on finding the one lost sheep that he leaves the ninety-nine in open country. We might presume that an undershepherd was left to guard them, but the story doesn't tell us that. In the parable, the owner of the sheep is so concerned for the loss of the one sheep that he can think of nothing but finding it. It doesn't say that he waited until someone came to watch the flock.

Imagine now for a moment that the lost sheep from the parable is your wayward son or daughter. God cares for them, just as the shepherd in the parable cares for his lost sheep. Prayerfully consider and hope for the day when the Lord saves your children—imagine Christ himself as the shepherd leading them home. Allow your hope in Christ and his power to save to bolster your flagging faith. We must maintain a strong faith that God can save our children and cast off unbelief.

It does us no good to look upon children lost in their sin and resign ourselves to the idea that they will never be saved. Your child may be lost, but that is the very criteria needed to qualify for God's salvation! Dare to believe, and keep believing that one day you will rejoice at the work of God in rescuing your lost children. On the day that they are saved, no one will rejoice more over their rescue than God himself. The greater the child's rebellion, the greater the repentance will be when God drops the blinders from his eyes and greater will be the rejoicing over his return.

Saving is the shepherd's work. That is why it is important not to fall into self-condemnation over our children's rebellion. Have our failures as parents contributed to their condition? Of course our sin affects our children. But God is able to save our children in spite of our failures.

So, you might ask, what if God doesn't save my son or daughter? We are tempted to doubt and the Enemy poses such questions to us all the time. But God never asks us to ponder, "What if my child will not be saved?" In the Scriptures, we are called to believe. God's hand is not too short to save (Isaiah 59:1), and he is able to save your son or daughter. So put your doubts to the side and dare to believe that your child is the next lost sheep on our Great Shepherd's list. Then pray again for her salvation and safe return with all your heart, and do so every day until she is returned to you.

Bring It Home

- Do you ever doubt God's ability or desire to save your children? How should this passage chase our doubts away?
- Confess your unbelief and ask God to help you trust in his ability to save your children, no matter how lost they may appear.

Day Three

The Lost Son

> And he said, "There was a man who had two sons. And the younger of them said to his father, 'Father, give me the share of property that is coming to me.' And he divided his property between them. Not many days later, the younger son gathered all he had and took a journey into a far country, and there he squandered his property in reckless living. And when he had spent everything, a severe famine arose in that country, and he began to be in need. So he went and hired himself out to one of the citizens of

that country, who sent him into his fields to feed pigs. And he was longing to be fed with the pods that the pigs ate, and no one gave him anything.

"But when he came to himself, he said, 'How many of my father's hired servants have more than enough bread, but I perish here with hunger! I will arise and go to my father, and I will say to him, "Father, I have sinned against heaven and before you. I am no longer worthy to be called your son. Treat me as one of your hired servants."' And he arose and came to his father. But while he was still a long way off, his father saw him and felt compassion, and ran and embraced him and kissed him. And the son said to him, 'Father, I have sinned against heaven and before you. I am no longer worthy to be called your son.' But the father said to his servants, 'Bring quickly the best robe, and put it on him, and put a ring on his hand, and shoes on his feet. And bring the fattened calf and kill it, and let us eat and celebrate. For this my son was dead, and is alive again; he was lost, and is found.' And they began to celebrate.

"Now his older son was in the field, and as he came and drew near to the house, he heard music and dancing. And he called one of the servants and asked what these things meant. And he said to him, 'Your brother has come, and your father has killed the fattened calf, because he has received him back safe and sound.' But he was angry and refused to go in. His father came out and entreated him, but he answered his father, 'Look, these many years I have served you, and I never disobeyed your command, yet you never gave me a young goat, that I might celebrate with my friends. But when this son of yours came, who has devoured your property with

prostitutes, you killed the fattened calf for him!' And
he said to him, 'Son, you are always with me, and all
that is mine is yours. It was fitting to celebrate and
be glad, for this your brother was dead, and is alive;
he was lost, and is found.'" (Luke 15:11–32)

Ponder Anew

The parable of the prodigal son has encouraged parents
with wayward children from the first day Jesus shared it. It is
hard to see our children leave home, deceived into believing
they will find happiness and fulfillment in the pleasures and
treasures of the world. The fearful reality is that the world is all
too happy to show them a good time, for a while. But the happiness they find apart from Christ in the pleasures of the world
is far from lasting joy.

While none of us wishes hurt upon our children, the trials
God designs to bring his children to their senses are a hardship
parents with wayward children should welcome, knowing God
is at work, bringing them to an end. Like the Prodigal Son in
the parable, who met his pigsty, let us place our hope in the
truth that God is in control and can create a trial designed to
bring our children home.

It is clear from reading the Prodigal Son's reflections that
his father was a fair and honest man, paying his servants generously. The son, having come now to his senses, has every
reason to believe that his father would welcome him home. He
needs only to repent. We detect no bitterness or relational bag-
gage in the story beyond the consequences brought on by the
prodigal's foolish behavior. In returning to his father's house,
he doesn't expect to go back as a son; he plans to ask for a place
among the servants.

We see from the story that the father has been waiting
for the day his son would crest the furthest hilltop. He hasn't

allowed his disappointment and grief to turn to bitterness. So, when his son appears far in the distance, he is the first to notice. He sets custom and decorum aside and runs to welcome him home.

It is important to note that the son is not returning to restock his moneybags, only to leave again. The words, "Father, I have sinned against heaven" demonstrate a godly sorrow which indicates that the son has wrestled with God and God has won. While there is a time for tough love, let us pray that when our children return repentant, we will welcome their phone call, text, email, or knock at the door. If they have not yet left, let us demonstrate such love that, if they do leave, they always know that help is a phone call away.

The father in the parable does more than embrace his son. He calls for a feast and welcomes him back into the family by awarding him a robe and a ring. From there, the parable turns a corner. God is also at work in the older son. The return of his younger brother, welcomed with open arms by his father, is the custom trial God designed to get at the elder brother's heart. The whole incident reveals the older brother's hidden rebellion, which is no less sinful before God than his younger brother's sin. Sadly, the story ends before we see any repentance from the older son. But rather than write him off, let's believe that the love of his father will be used by God to draw him home as well.

The older brother represents the Pharisees, who criticized Jesus for eating with sinners and hanging with the lost. But even the self-righteous Pharisees could be saved. Let's hope that, if one of our children resembles the older son, he would repent as Nicodemus did, who sought the Lord (John 3) and accompanied Joseph of Arimathea to bury our Lord (John 19:39). Though he was a Pharisee, he identified with Jesus in his death, having repented of his sin.

When our children pack their bags and run from home, or reject God's grace in their stubborn pride, we need not fear. Let us look to heaven and ask our sovereign Lord to release the trial he has composed for them, that they might return to him and us. While we wait and pray for their return, let us soak in the deep mercies God has extended to us through the cross so that when we are met with our son's or daughter's repentance, our response will match that of the father in the parable.

Bring It Home

- How are you encouraged by the parable of the prodigal son? In what ways are you challenged by the father's response to the son?
- What Scriptures illustrating God's mercy can keep you anchored in Christ, avoiding bitterness when your children rebel? If you can't think of any, do an internet search for the top ten Scriptures on the mercy of God. Choose a few to memorize.

Real Life

Jim and Barb followed the biblical course laid out for parenting their children, training them up in the way they should go. They trusted that if they discipled their children in the things of the Lord, all would be well. They expected trials but were unprepared for the abject rebellion of their second-born daughter Cathleen. Looking back, they not only see the hand of God at work in their daughter, they also see how God taught them to depend on him rather than trust in faithful parenting to save their daughter.

Cathleen made a profession of faith in high school and was baptized, but her life quickly started to veer away from faith around the time she dropped out of college. It was then that Cathleen traded the pursuit of God to chase after the pleasures of the world. She separated herself from all appeals to God and wisdom and got her own place to do what she wanted. When she announced that she was leaving the area with her live-in boyfriend to return to his home city, the news crushed Jim and Barb. It seemed as though all their past parenting efforts had failed them. Now all they could do was trust the Lord for their daughter.

Somehow, with Cathleen far away, Jim felt more helpless. He lay on his pillow at night, not knowing where she was or what she was doing. The story of the prodigal son often came to mind as he wrestled with the fact that the daughter he had prayed for all her life was gone. The prodigal who came to his senses and repented while feeding the pigs helped Jim keep his head above water and hold fast to hope. He prayed that God would grant the same repentance to Cathleen.

I had first met Cathleen when she served on our children's ministry drama team. She was a talented actress and gave herself to the gospel skits we performed for the grade school kids. I lost regular contact with her family after they were sent out with a church plant. So I was sad to later learn she had left home and wasn't following the Lord. It wasn't until a few years later when Cathleen returned to share her testimony that I discovered the details of her rescue.

Cathleen, like so many children who stray, felt judged by the church. It was, in fact, God's law that judged her. So, to escape the rules and the scrutiny she felt were keeping her from being fulfilled and happy, she left home. "I entered a season of purposeful rebellion against the church, my parents, and God himself," she said of those early days of her turning from God.

Distraught, Jim and Barb met with another couple from their church at the recommendation of their pastor. They had been through a similar experience with their daughter. Their advice was, "Just keep loving her, just keep loving her." Jim and Barb did their best to take that advice, and though they grieved, they sought to prevent their grief from spilling over into bitterness—or worse, self-righteousness.

Off in the big city, Cathleen got engaged to her boyfriend, but that did not last. She began dating her boss, a much older man and a self-made millionaire who showered her with all the glitz this world had to offer. Despite the pleading words of caution from family and friends, the truth they shared did not reach her stone-cold conscience. But she soon discovered that her boss had a dark side. He was frighteningly possessive and emotionally abusive toward her. The freedom she wanted from the rules of home and church had led her to a trap and a cage of her own making. Still, she stubbornly refused to confess her sin, repent, and return to her family.

"On Tuesday, December 2," Cathleen shared, "while I was drowning in my sin, God in his mercy sent me a life raft in the form of two tiny pink lines that appeared on a pregnancy test." Cathleen knew she had two options. She could call her family, admit her sin, and move back home. Or, she could end the life of her child to keep the favor of her boss, the glitz, and the worldly wealth he promised to award her.

Three days later, unable to shake a deeply held value for all human life—a truth passed on to her from her parents—Cathleen chose life. She humbled herself and asked her dad to come and get her.

Jim was on another call when he saw his daughter's name on the screen. He wrapped up his call and quickly answered. Instinctively, he knew Cathleen was in trouble. His response to his daughter's news was, "It's okay. It's okay. I'm coming to get you." Those words demonstrated his fatherly love. He told Cathleen he would call her back as soon as he figured out the details. Jim immediately called Barb and gave her the news. As they wrestled for wisdom, Jim remembered assuring his wife, "I don't know what God is doing. All I know is I've got to go get her." He left immediately and called Cathleen several times on the trip. Jim didn't get to Cathleen's place until late that night. He loaded her things into the family minivan and left the city as fast as his conscience would allow him to fly. "I felt like a paratrooper on a mission," he remembered. Looking back, even in those early moments of rescue, Jim saw the first glimmers of grace—God was working in his daughter's heart.

Cathleen shared in her testimony the effect of her dad's loving actions. "It was a Thursday afternoon," Cathleen recalled. "He dropped everything he was doing and drove sixteen hours to pick me up and bring me home. This action of my dad was the first of many ways that God started to show me that true love is merciful and sacrificial."

Cathleen's parents welcomed her home. She feared that the church would scorn and reject her, but that was not the case at all. The church, along with her family, gave her a beautiful baby shower. She received all the baby supplies she needed, along with countless cards and financial support. Her mom became her biggest advocate and was there during the delivery of her son Dominic.

Motherhood wasn't easy for Cathleen, but it taught her that love is about sacrifice. Reflecting on God's plan to save her, Cathleen shared, "God knew that my pregnancy would be the only thing to stop me in my tracks and turn me back in the direction of truth. I shudder to think of the person I would be today if I'd made the ultimate choice to throw my son's life away. God used my unplanned pregnancy as the means to change my belief that Christianity is a religion of laws into a belief that I serve a personal God and a merciful Savior."

Cathleen recalled that, in all her disobedience, she knew that with one phone call home to her parents, everything would be alright. She didn't doubt their love or their unwavering convictions and knew that they would support her decision to keep her son. That assurance bolstered her courage to make that call. In the end, God used Jim and Barb's parenting—the value they passed on to their daughter regarding the sanctity of life—to save her. God has a way of humbling us as parents to depend on him, but once we cling to him, he uses our labors for good in the life of our children.

Cathleen finished telling her story at our church by sharing what she learned through her experience. "I stand here today a believer in three things. First, no matter the circumstances from which a pregnancy is conceived, life is always a gift. My son, Dominic, is a huge testament to that reality. Secondly, God's promises are true, and the choice to obey him will always result in blessing. Thirdly, the lies of this world are lies, and a sinful choice can never result in happiness. Only by clinging to Christ's goodness, imputed to me on the cross, can I change from the person I have been and become truly fulfilled."

The day Cathleen turned from her sin, all heaven rejoiced, and the Great Shepherd who sought out this lost sheep celebrated the loudest. Back on earth, her family is still rejoicing.

CHAPTER 13

Refined by God

1 Peter 1:3–12

Introduction to the Week

Parenting trials come in all shapes and sizes. God uses the unexpected to build our faith and has uniquely fashioned trials for each of us. Kimberly Fugate was surprised to find out that she was two months pregnant at age forty-one; she would be forty-two when she gave birth. Then, a day before her forty-second birthday, well into her pregnancy, Kimberly discovered that she and her husband, Craig, weren't having one, but three babies. Then, at twenty-eight weeks, Kimberly went into labor. It ended in a caesarean section, when doctors discovered a fourth baby girl, all identical from a single egg.

Kimberly was working two jobs when she found out that she was pregnant. With quadruplets weighing in at just over two pounds each and thirteen weeks premature, she wasn't even able to hold her "sweet miracles." They were in isolation. How would she afford to clothe and feed the four girls, let alone pay for the four thousand diapers she would go through in a year? As the tiny girls struggled for life, calls for prayer went out—and people prayed.

Their home church, Calvary Temple Pentecostal, hosted a county-wide baby shower and the Lord provided for their needs. All four girls made it home and are doing well. Reflecting back on their first birthday celebration for an interview, Kimberly didn't complain about the difficulties or the thousands of changed diapers. Kimberly recognized God's hand in her 13 million-to-one chance pregnancy. "I believed that God picked me to have these quadruplets, and I felt that he would take care of them and allow them to survive. To see how far they've come makes me feel very blessed."[1]

Knowing that God is behind our unique parenting trials can help us get through the hardest nights. Parenting trials come in all shapes and sizes, but the one thing they have in common is the stretching and refining of the faith of the parents who endure them. Whatever your parenting trial, you can know that God is at work behind the scenes. God is doing more than raising children through our parenting. He is also shaping us. Laura Story's song, "Blessings,"[2] captures well the multifaceted purposes of God, using our trials to draw us to himself. Laura asks a poignant question which affected me as I was writing this chapter and heard the song play on the radio. What if life's most difficult moments are really God's disguised blessings to keep us from loving the world more than we love him? I am convinced that if God gave me a trial-free life, I would not know the deep fellowship I've experienced with God, seeing my weakness exposed through the trials of my life. I think that is true for most of us.

Day One

Tested by the Fire of Our Trials

> Blessed be the God and Father of our Lord Jesus
> Christ! According to his great mercy, he has caused

---

1. https://www.littlethings.com/mom-surprise-quadruplets-kimberly/
2. "Blessings" by Laura Story, INO records, 2011.

us to be born again to a living hope through the resurrection of Jesus Christ from the dead, to an inheritance that is imperishable, undefiled, and unfading,
kept in heaven for you, who by God's power are
being guarded through faith for a salvation ready
to be revealed in the last time. In this you rejoice,
though now for a little while, if necessary, you have
been grieved by various trials, so that the tested genuineness of your faith—more precious than gold that
perishes though it is tested by fire—may be found to
result in praise and glory and honor at the revelation
of Jesus Christ. (1 Peter 1:3–7)

Ponder Anew

Few Bible passages better speak to our parenting trials than
1 Peter 1. Peter opens his epistle by announcing our great,
imperishable salvation in Christ to help put our earthly trials
into perspective. Peter speaks from his experience. The night of
Christ's arrest, he thought he could conquer the world at Jesus's
side. He had boasted of his loyalty, "Even if I have to die with
you, I will never disown you" (Matthew 26:35 NIV). Unfortunately for Peter, his confidence rested on himself instead of
God. God would use the subsequent trial to reorient Peter's
priorities.

After leaving the upper room with Jesus and the disciples
for the Garden of Gethsemane, Peter soon found out what a
defining trial feels like. Though he had been warned by Jesus
that Satan wanted to sift him like wheat, he didn't take the
warning seriously and couldn't stay awake to pray.

Later, when the soldiers came to arrest Jesus, Peter went on
the offensive. He drew his sword and cut off the ear of the high
priest's servant. Imagine his surprise when Jesus didn't join the
fight. Jesus didn't call down fire from heaven or enlist armies of

angels to join the attack. Instead, Jesus rebuked Peter, told him to put away his sword, and gave himself up for arrest. Peter's trial of fire had begun; Jesus's arrest rocked his world. Peter fell into the trap Satan had laid for him. He ran. When later confronted, he denied Jesus three times, just as Jesus had warned. The cock's crow became judge and jury over Peter, rendering a verdict of guilty in the courts of heaven. Then the crucifixion ended his hopes that Jesus would usher the nation of Israel into a new Davidic dynasty. Peter hit bottom. God designed the whole trial to help Peter see his need for a Savior and it worked as planned. The night's events shattered his self-confidence and exposed his sin and need for a Savior. Peter withdrew and wept bitterly. While the words he prayed are not recorded for us, it is easy to imagine that he cried out to God for help and forgiveness and repented of his independent pride.

Then, on the third day, Jesus rose from the dead, and subsequently sought Peter out. Jesus forgave and restored Peter and commissioned him to "feed his sheep." He once again spoke the words "Follow me" (John 21:19), which welcomed Peter back as a disciple in good standing. From that point on, Peter's confidence remained in Christ. His life took on renewed meaning. He took the lead at Pentecost, boldly proclaiming the gospel publicly. Peter was back in renewed boldness, but he never forgot the trial the Lord used to refine him. We see the backdrop of that trial in our passage today. As we approach the book of 1 Peter, let's do so knowing that the man who is encouraging us to see God's fingerprints on our trials is speaking from experience.

God remains in complete control over every detail of our lives, just as he was over every detail of Peter's life. He knew Peter's trial from start to finish before it took place. Satan needed God's permission to test Peter. And God worked everything together for good in Peter's life. God does the same for us.

Peter describes our earthly trials as lasting "for a little while." One day, when we've reached heaven, we'll look back and consider the longest of our trials as "momentary" (2 Corinthians 4:17). That is because eternity brings perspective on our present trials. Our trials are but a flash in the pan compared to an eternity with God in a restored world, where all sorrow, sin, and trial are gone. Just as a soldier must endure two months of hard training in boot camp, designed to prepare him for life in the armed forces, so we live our lives in this earthly training ground to prepare us for an eternity in heaven. Keeping at least one eye focused on heaven can help us find the strength to praise God for the challenges we face and bear up under them.

As Christians who have been born again, Peter tells us that we enter a "living hope." Even if we die, we know we will live forever. God made this promise and guards it so that we can never lose our inheritance. Our failure can't corrupt it, the enemy cannot steal it away, and the promise will never fade. One day, when the Lord re-creates the earth, we will live and walk this planet trial-free with Jesus.

We must consider our present trials with these deep but wonderful truths as a backdrop. Looking ahead to a trial-free eternity causes our earthly trials to shrink. Peter also reveals the purpose behind our trials. Our hardships are not random, limitless, or uncontrolled. They've been designed and allowed by God to refine our faith and prepare us for an eternity with Jesus.

Raw gold ore is dug up from the earth, crushed, sluiced to remove the waste, rock, and mud, and then placed in a crucible and heated to its melting point. Then the dross is removed, and the remaining pure gold poured into an ingot. To form a wedding ring, the ingot is melted again and cast into a circle, then hammered, filed, and polished. The raw gold bound to the impurities of stone endures quite a trial to become a wedding ring ready for that final celebration. God is likewise working through our trials to refine us so that one day we shine and reflect the image of our Creator, much like a ring captures the image of the jeweler who looks upon it.

Bring It Home

- How can putting our present trials in perspective against an eternity of trial-free life with Jesus give us strength and faith to endure today?
- Write out a prayer that asks God to help you in your trials but also asks the Lord to increase your longing for heaven and a day when your present trials are over.

Day Two

Faith for Rejoicing

> Though you have not seen him, you love him. Though you do not now see him, you believe in him and rejoice with joy that is inexpressible and filled with glory, obtaining the outcome of your faith, the salvation of your souls. (1 Peter 1:8–9)

Ponder Anew

In 1 Peter 1:3–7, Peter contrasted our earthly trials with our eternal, unperishable salvation in heaven. We learned that every trial we face is put to work by God to build our faith and refine us like gold, for a future day when we will see Jesus face to face and live with him forever. In that day, we'll look back and see how God used the trials in our parenting for our good and his glory. Our faith will be strong for having walked through them.

God is refining us so that our faith will be found genuine and result in praise (see v. 7). Peter is so confident in God's ability to refine our faith that he speaks a declaration of love on our behalf:

> Though you have not seen him, you love him. Though you do not now see him, you believe in him and rejoice with joy that is inexpressible and filled with glory, obtaining the outcome of your faith, the salvation of your souls. (v. 8)

While we may not feel much like rejoicing in the middle of a difficult parenting trial, we can trust God to use our challenges to refine us (and our child) so that the declaration Peter spoke over our lives is true. While our trials can at times seem unbearable, we can rejoice in remembering that God loves us and has prepared a place for us. We can rejoice in knowing that he works all things together for our good and will not allow us to be tempted beyond what we can bear. So call out to God in the midst of your trial. Tell him that you love and trust him with your life and that you know he will accomplish his purpose through your trials while also guarding your salvation.

One day, we will see how God worked our trials together for our good, and we will see how our one thread was woven into God's larger kingdom tapestry. Close up, we are just a thread, but from the perspective of eternity, we will be able to view the whole fabric and marvel at the way he used us and our children for his purpose and glory and our good. Oh, Christian parent, believe that your children will be standing next to you on that day! Just as God is able to work your trials for good, he is also able to bring them the trials that will perfect their faith as well. Stand in faith and believe that on that day, we will stand with our children and join the chorus in celebration of our God.

Isaac Watts put Peter's exhortation to music in his hymn, "Blest be the Everlasting God."

> To an inheritance divine
> he taught our hearts to rise;
> 'tis uncorrupted, undefiled,
> unfading in the skies.
>
> Saints by the power of God are kept,
> till the salvation come:
> we walk by faith as strangers here,
> but Christ shall call us home.[3]

Bring It Home

- How is God refining you through your trials? What areas of sin is he seeking to remove? What grace is he interested in adding to your character? Rather than fight against this process, welcome it in prayer before God.
- Call out to the Lord, personalizing 1 Peter 1:8–9 to tell the Lord of your love for him. It is a holy thing for us to praise God as we endure our trials and to celebrate his goodness even while we struggle through doubts.

Day Three

The Prophets Longed for Christ

Concerning this salvation, the prophets who prophesied about the grace that was to be yours searched and inquired carefully, inquiring what person or time the Spirit of Christ in them was indicating when he predicted the sufferings of Christ and the

---

3. Isaac Watts, *Hymns and Spiritual Songs, Book I*, 1707, number 26.

subsequent glories. It was revealed to them that they were serving not themselves but you, in the things that have now been announced to you through those who preached the good news to you by the Holy Spirit sent from heaven, things into which angels long to look. (1 Peter 1:10–12)

Ponder Anew

The average Christian home has upwards of a dozen Bibles sitting on nightstands and bookshelves. Many Christians have read through the Bible multiple times. We skim through the most incredible stories, truths, and revelations of God. But there is no greater revelation than knowing Jesus. When Christians are caught in a difficult trial, they often say, "How do people do it without the Lord?" Well, imagine the prophets. They endured the same trials of life we do, yet saw but a shadow of Christ. They longed to know what we are privileged to see and understand with clarity.

They were given bits and pieces and clues, which they studied carefully, trying to discern who and when and how God would restore his kingdom. They wondered intently, Who would God's Messiah be?

Think of it this way. They had parenting trials like the rest of us. Their kids disobeyed and rebelled. Their children refused to go to worship and gave themselves over to the world and its pleasures. But none of them had Jesus. They had a future hope, and by trusting in that future hope, they were saved. Still, none of them knew the cross, the one final sacrifice for sin. None knew the resurrection, nor did they have 1 Peter 1 to know that God was using their trials to refine them.

The animal sacrifices they offered in faith celebrated God's mercy and forgiveness. They trusted in a future Redeemer and longed for his coming. Even the little prophetic truth God gave them was revealed to them so that they might speak it for our benefit—that we might go back to the book of Isaiah and read his prophecies to help us believe. Today, in contrast, we hold the Gospels' detailed accounts of his life in our hands.

In light of this, it is important to see what a travesty it would be for us to glance over 1 Peter 1 casually and not allow it to affect our souls. Consider Peter's words and the truth they reveal again: "He has caused us to be born again to a living hope through the resurrection of Jesus Christ from the dead, to an inheritance that is imperishable, undefiled, and unfading, kept in heaven for you, who by God's power are being guarded through faith for a salvation ready to be revealed in the last time" (1 Peter 1:3–5).

As for our trials? The apostle Paul, agreeing with Peter, sums it up this way:

> So we do not lose heart. Though our outer self is wasting away, our inner self is being renewed day by day. For this light momentary affliction is preparing for us an eternal weight of glory beyond all comparison, as we look not to the things that are seen but to the things that are unseen. For the things that are seen are transient, but the things that are unseen are eternal. (2 Corinthians 4:16–18)

Bring It Home

- How are Paul's words in 2 Corinthians 4:16–18 similar to what Peter said in 1 Peter 1:3–7?
- How are you encouraged by Peter's words in 1 Peter 1:10–12 and Paul's words in 2 Corinthians 4:16–18?

Real Life

While working on this manuscript, I came across the contract New Growth Press offered me for the project. There are two names at the bottom of the signature page: mine as the author and that of the Editorial Director for New Growth Press, Barbara Juliani. Barbara enthusiastically supported *Parenting First Aid* from the first day she read my proposal. Her encouragement and helpful critique in previous books have been used of God to grow my writing skills.

Barbara is more than a wordsmith. She knows her Bible and knows how to communicate complex theological concepts in ways the average reader can understand. That has served many an author. Soon after meeting Barbara, I learned that she grew up in a theologically-minded home. Her father, Jack Miller, was a seminary professor, pastor, missionary, and author. It is evident that he passed his skills and gifts on to his daughter.

Imagine my surprise when I discovered that my theologically astute editor was herself a prodigal daughter. At the height of her running from God, she found herself trapped in a live-in relationship with a big-time drug dealer, surrounded by stacks of money, guns, fast cars, and more than a dozen guard dogs. I marveled at God's work as I read her story in the book Barbara co-authored with her father, *Come Back, Barbara*. Their story confirmed the lessons God was teaching me at the time—that he uses our parenting trials to refine the faith of Mom and Dad.

The fireworks began in the Miller household when eighteen-year-old Barbara announced to her parents, "I don't want to act like a Christian anymore! And I am not going to!"[4] "Barbara wanted freedom—freedom from all constraints, from parents, from church, from God. She was after the happiness

---

4. C. John Miller and Barbara Miller Juliani, *Come Back, Barbara Second Edition* (Phillipsburg, NJ: P&R Publishing 1997), 21.

that she sensed was to be found 'out there,' apart from home and Christianity, and she wanted to be happy *now*."[5]

Barbara's independence and search for happiness led her to romance. Soon she was living with her boyfriend. That caused a stir back home. God was using Barbara's rebellion to humble her parents and refine their faith. Learning to love a daughter who so thoroughly cast off her upbringing wasn't easy. But God was faithful to teach Jack and Rose Marie how to trust God with Barbara and learn to love her despite her sin; the kind of love God demonstrated toward them.

Before long, Barbara was married, but without Christ. She soon left her husband for the elusive fulfillment she longed for and the marriage ended in divorce. Like the nation of Israel, each time God disciplined her through trial, Barbara returned home. But without true repentance, the world quickly drew her back. It was several years and men later before his refining work in her and her parents was complete. By that time, God brought a guy named Angelo into her life to play an important role in his redemptive plan for her life.

Even though they were not believers and not serving the Lord, the church back home collected over eight hundred dollars to help them move to California, where Barbara planned to begin a Ph.D. program at Stanford. The money, along with a stack of encouraging notes, cracked Angelo's stony heart. He gave his life to Christ after attending church the next Easter, a few weeks after he and Barbara were married.

Just before leaving for Stanford, Jack lovingly challenged his daughter with the gospel. Her flesh didn't want to listen, but God was slowly opening her spiritual eyes. Once in California, Barbara began to read the Bible—not exactly proper liberal etiquette! Finally, after years of running from God, she succumbed to the gospel love she saw in Scripture, and she

5. Ibid., 25.

too bowed her knee. In time God called Angelo into the ministry. His ordination as a pastor demonstrated God's awesome redemption and just a bit of humor. Barbara had vowed that she would never marry a pastor. That didn't mean God couldn't transform her dishonest, drug-dealing boyfriend into one!

Through those refining years, Jack and Rose Marie learned to "talk less about their problems and pray more."[6] They learned to entrust their daughter to God and keep out of the way of his work, showing her an enduring love that wasn't based on her good behavior. They discovered that God's refining wasn't just for their daughter; he was after their hearts too and wanted to uproot their self-righteousness. In their book, Jack remembered, "More than once he let us see that we needed to be rescued as much as Barbara did—perhaps even more since there is no more impenetrable barrier to God's love that the sense of being right. So often self-righteousness controls a parent's attitudes toward a rebellious offspring."[7] In the end, it was the refining work in her parents that God used to demonstrate biblical love to his lost daughter.

Today, thousands of parents with rebellious children have been encouraged by their testimony. And it was their son and Barbara's brother, Paul Miller, who wrote the book, *A Praying Life*, that so affected me. Clearly, he learned from watching their example. One day in heaven, we'll all share our stories of God's refining work in us and our kids. For now, it can be encouragement enough to know that you are not alone. God is in control, using every trial to build your faith and help you find your hope in him.

6. Miller and Juliani, *Come Back, Barbara*, 46.
7. Ibid., 150.

CHAPTER 14

He Knows
that We Are Dust

Psalm 103

Introduction to the Week

I recently flew over a wealthy golf course neighborhood. Its enormous mansions seemed like toys from several thousand feet up in the sky. Up there, I saw their relative insignificance in the overall landscape. And if I'd flown higher, the smaller those stately homes would appear. Even our solar system is small compared to the whole Milky Way galaxy, with its 100 billion stars. And beyond that, the Milky Way is minuscule compared to the known universe with its 100+ billion galaxies.

Going in the opposite direction, the mansion I observed from the plane is huge in comparison to the people who live in it. We all are huge compared to one of the thirty trillion cells that make up the average human body. Yet that cell is enormous compared to the two trillion molecules which form it. And beyond that, every molecule is constructed from multiple atoms, which are made up of smaller protons, neutrons, electrons, and quarks, which, compared to the universe, are immeasurably small.

To help us see how insignificant our efforts are compared to God's great mercy and compassion, the Spirit of God inspired the writer of Psalm 103 to describe us as "dust." While that may seem like an insulting comparison, it is actually one of the most encouraging poetic phrases in the Psalms. For if God knows that all our talents and efforts have as much impact as dust, then surely he also knows that we need his compassion, mercy, and love.

Day One

A Command to Oneself

> Bless the LORD, O my soul, and all that is within me, bless his holy name! Bless the LORD, O my soul, and forget not all his benefits, who forgives all your iniquity, who heals all your diseases, who redeems your life from the pit, who crowns you with steadfast love and mercy, who satisfies you with good so that your youth is renewed like the eagle's. (Psalm 103:1–5)

Ponder Anew

The great nineteenth-century preacher Charles Spurgeon considered Psalm 103 the greatest of the psalms. His poetic description of the song, which he attributed to David, ascends as close to divinely inspired language as any human words have risen.

> As in the lofty Alps some peaks rise above all others, so among even the inspired Psalms there are heights of song which overtop the rest. This one hundred and third Psalm has ever seemed to us to be the Monte Rosa of the divine chain of mountains of praise, glowing with a ruddier light than any of the rest. It is as the apple tree among the trees of the

wood, and its golden fruit has a flavour such as no fruit ever bears unless it has been ripened in the full sunshine of mercy. It is man's reply to the benedictions of his God, his Song on the Mount answering to his Redeemer's Sermon on the Mount.[1]

There is too much in the Psalm for a thousand pens to write; it is one of those all-comprehending Scriptures which is a Bible in itself, and it might alone almost suffice for the hymn-book of the church.[2]

Assuming the good preacher is correct about the author of Psalm 103, David speaks to our troubles with truth after glorious truth in this wonderful song. He aims to lift our eyes from our troubles toward the heavens, to gaze upon our beautiful God. He begins by issuing a command to himself: "Bless the LORD, O my soul." Once is not enough; he again orders his soul to "Bless the LORD." Then he quickly moves on to the reason for our hope—the blessings and promises of God that begin with forgiveness.

As glorious, and encouraging as the message of Psalm 103 is, our Enemy would try and distract us from such rich truth by keeping our eyes focused on our troubles. Don't listen to him if, while you are reading the Scriptures, he tempts you to think instead of your troubles and convince you that the mercies described in the song don't apply to you.

If ever our earthly troubles or the Enemy's temptations drag us down, we should remember that we are forgiven. The implications of our forgiveness are encouraging beyond measure. Since God sent his only Son to die to remove our sins, we have every reason to believe and expect the stated blessings of this psalm. So use the truth of your redemption to cast

---

1. Charles Spurgeon, *Treasury of David*, Volume 2 (Peabody: Hendrickson Publishers, 1996), 275.
2. Ibid.

off the lies of the Enemy, which seek to keep you in the pit of doubt and despair. Then, like the psalmist, command your soul to bless the Lord and forget not all his benefits. Cry out to God and thank him for your salvation, redemption, adoption, future resurrection, and the restoration of all things.

What does it mean to have your youth renewed like the eagles? The prophet Isaiah sheds light on this question when he wrote, "Those who hope in the LORD will renew their strength. They will soar on wings like eagles; they will run and not grow weary, they will walk and not be faint" (Isaiah 40:31 NIV). When an eagle tires, like other great soaring birds, it needs simply to capture a thermal. The hot air rising from the sun-warmed earth lifts the majestic bird to lofty heights without a single flap of its wings. The warm updraft signals to the weary raptor that no more exertion is needed. Similarly, the promises of Psalm 103 are meant to be our updraft of grace. Soar on the promise that you are forgiven, that God is willing to heal, pour out his love and mercy upon you, and satisfy you with good. To believe the words of the psalmist allows you to stop your tired labors and simply spread your wings to fly. While you rest in God's grace, you are taken higher and receive needed rest for your weary soul.

Bring It Home

- What lies and discouragements does the Enemy use to keep you focused on your troubles?
- Have you ever noticed that we must take our eyes off God to focus on our troubles? Make a list of all your troubles, then fold it up and put it aside. Read through Psalm 103 aloud. Speak the words of the psalm out loud and up to the heavens as your prayer. Then ask God to renew your faith and strength and take the burden of your troubles away.

Day Two

An All-Important Word

> The LORD works righteousness and justice for all who are oppressed. He made known his ways to Moses, his acts to the people of Israel. The LORD is merciful and gracious, slow to anger and abounding in steadfast love. He will not always chide, nor will he keep his anger forever. He does not deal with us according to our sins, nor repay us according to our iniquities. (Psalm 103:6–10)

Ponder Anew

In the midst of Israel's greatest sin, God described himself to Moses using the words that appear in verse 8. After pleading with God not to withdraw his presence from Israel after their idolatry in making the golden calf, Moses asks to see God in all his glory (Exodus 33:18). But since no man can see God and live, the Lord tells Moses that he will instead allow all his goodness to pass before Moses and then declare his name to him. God then passes before Moses, who is safely hidden in the cleft of a rock, and speaks his name, adding the words the psalmist repeats in verse 8. This description of God is repeated more than thirty times in over a dozen books of the Bible. It is worth committing to memory.

Still, encouraging Scriptures like Psalm 103 can be difficult to embrace when life doesn't line up with the blessings we see in the text. When the experiences of our lives seem to belie the promises of Scripture, it is easy to become discouraged and wrongfully assume that the promises are not for you. You believe in the idea that you are forgiven and redeemed, but your daily experience battling your sin or that of your children doesn't seem to mesh with the promises. Or perhaps you've prayed for God's healing with no relief, and you can't remember the last time you felt like your strength was renewed like an eagle's. What then?

The Enemy and our flesh are ever ready to discount eternal truths based on our current experience, to get our eyes off God's promises and focus on today's troubles. The psalmist anticipates the doubts that life's trials bring and the condemnation that the Enemy is ever ready to heap upon us. Comfort comes from studying God's words and asking the Holy Spirit to help you trust that they are true for you. When it says, "The LORD works righteousness and justice for all who are oppressed," that word "all" includes you, whether you feel like it or not.

Should the Enemy taunt you with condemnation and hold verse 9 over your head—"See, God is chiding you, he is angry with you and therefore will not give you the promises"—remember that the words of verse 8 were first given to Israel in the midst of their worst sin. Then allow the words of verse 10 to rescue you: "He does not deal with us according to our sins, nor repay us according to our iniquities." Our punishment was poured out on Christ. Yes, God does use trials to perfect us, but we have already seen that these are the disciplines of a loving Father, not retribution for our failures. Our God is merciful and gracious, slow to anger, and abounding in steadfast love. So don't listen to the Enemy. Your present trials are not punishment from God for your failures. And the promises of God are yours to believe.

One day all evil and all suffering will be removed and our last tear wiped away. As a redeemed child of God, you will live to see that day. Listen to the apostle John describe it.

> And I heard a loud voice from the throne saying, "Behold, the dwelling place of God is with man. He will dwell with them, and they will be his people,

and God himself will be with them as their God. He will wipe away every tear from their eyes, and death shall be no more, neither shall there be mourning, nor crying, nor pain anymore, for the former things have passed away." (Revelation 21:3–4)

The reality that your present trials are difficult must not rob you of the hope and encouragement God intends for your soul through this psalm. The Lord will work righteousness and justice on your behalf. He is working now, and whatever trials he allows today for your growth and your good he will one day banish forever.

Bring It Home

- Review Hebrews 12:3–12. What is the difference between the punishment of God for our sin and the loving discipline of the Lord? Why is it important to keep the Hebrews 12 passage in mind when we read Psalm 103?
- How does remembering the cross add weight to the words, "So great is his steadfast love toward those who fear him"? How can we use the truth of Psalm 103:10 to help us when the Enemy condemns us?

Day Three

What Can Dust Do on Its Own?

For as high as the heavens are above the earth, so great is his steadfast love toward those who fear him; as far as the east is from the west, so far does he remove our transgressions from us. As a father shows compassion to his children, so the LORD shows compassion

to those who fear him. For he knows our frame; he
remembers that we are dust. (Psalm 103:11–15)

Ponder Anew

Few illustrations demonstrate love more than a father lovingly helping his young child. Picture a little boy who can't
reach the water fountain. He looks up to his dad and says,
"Can you help me?" The father lifts his son lovingly and holds
him secure for as long as it takes to quench his thirst. Or imagine a dad helping his daughter ride a bicycle. He holds her
steady, gives her a gentle push, and then runs alongside her to
catch her should she lose her balance. That is a picture of God's
love and compassion for us. His love is so great for us that it is
as big as heaven is high above the earth.

While the author of Psalm 103 understood that the love of
God is best illustrated by his removal of our transgressions, it
was not until God sent his Son that the full extent of his great
love was revealed. "For God so loved the world, that he gave his
only Son" (John 3:16). How do you describe the immeasurably
great love that is demonstrated in a Father offering his Son to
die as a substitute for another? Jesus took the punishment we
deserved upon himself so that we could be forgiven. So how
forgiven are we? We are infinitely forgiven—as far as the east is
from the west!

If ever you were tempted to think that God looks down
upon you with disappointment, remember that you are infinitely forgiven. Speak verse 15 back to yourself: "He knows my
frame; he remembers that I am dust." All dust can do is mess
things up! If you clean your house and put all in order before a
vacation, dust will fall while you are away, requiring you clean
all over again upon your return. Dust is not like the colorful
green patina of corroded bronze; dust never adds beauty. No
one says, "I can't wait till our new furniture develops a coating

of fine dust." So rejoice in this truth: Whenever God looks down at our capacity to change our own hearts or the hearts of our children, he remembers our frame and knows that we are dust. When it comes to providing for your family, leading them spiritually, making the right choices, solving your marriage difficulties, and any of a hundred other responsibilities, we need God and he knows that we need him.

If there was ever an area of life that makes us feel like dust, it is reaching our kids with the gospel. We share the words, but so often they seem to fall to the ground with no effect. At that moment we must remember that it is not up to us. We are called to share the words of life, but God is the Author of life, who promises to make the words we share effective in the lives of our kids. When it comes to transforming the lives of our children, our frames are weak. We are dust and need our mighty God to move on our behalf. If you've shared the gospel with your children but they seem unaffected, do not give up hope, for God can cause the seed of the gospel to sprout, years later, even after you've gone.

While we may be dust standing alone in our own strength, we do not stand alone. God is with us. The Spirit of God lives inside our hearts. His presence within us changes everything. When we face the challenges of the day, we need not depend on our mortal frame or strength. We can call upon the Spirit of God. We do so with the confidence that God will answer us because of his enormous love and compassion toward us. God knows that we can't do life on our own and is ready to help us. And of course, he knows he must, for what can dust do on its own?

Bring It Home

- What most encourages you from Psalm 103?
- When faced with challenges, do you focus on your human ability alone to solve your problems or do you

remember that the Spirit of God is with you to help you face the difficulties of the day?
- Call out to the Spirit of God and ask for help for today.

Real Life

It was a typical Friday night after my daughter Emma attended her weekly worship and prayer meeting at Destin's house. Emma and her friend Lindsay remained after the rest of the crowd left to give Emma time to visit with Destin and his mother Maria, who hosted the meeting. They enjoyed talking about the amazing ways God was touching people's lives and drawing them into his kingdom. They often took some time to pray for friends who still needed Jesus. On this evening, Destin turned the corner of their conversation by asking, "Who should we pray for?" Lindsay didn't hesitate to answer. "Can we pray for my sister Kelsey? I just want God to save her." The four of them then spent some time interceding for Kelsey. Moments after they said the final "Amen," Lindsay's phone rang. It was Kelsey, who was finishing up a late shift at work. Kelsey felt an unusual prompting at that moment to call her sister, something she never did at that hour.

Before their conversation ended, Lindsay invited Kelsey to join her for breakfast the next morning. Kelsey agreed, but didn't know that Lindsay planned to take her to church for the buffet breakfast we served at our Bridge Course, an evangelistic introduction to Christianity scheduled to begin that next day. Lindsay still had to reveal that part of the plan to Kelsey, but the uncanny timing of the phone call told her and the others that God was answering their prayer.

Lindsay and Kelsey grew up in a Christian home, surrounded by their mom's strong faith, though their father Jack didn't become a Christian until they were out of grade school. For most of their upbringing, he struggled with alcoholism.

But once God opened his eyes to the truth of the gospel, Jack repented of his sin and his life dramatically changed. He stopped drinking and began to read the Bible, which Kelsey and Lindsay saw him study frequently. It seemed to them that he always had his Bible open. One of Jack's greatest desires was that his two daughters would turn from their sin and trust in Jesus.

Lindsay, who called herself a Christian, didn't follow the Lord at that point. But she loved her dad very much and purchased a legacy journal at the local gift shop as a birthday present for him. The journal was designed for fathers to write out their life story for their children. Jack saw it as an opportunity to pass the gospel to his daughters. He cherished the gift and took seriously the task of answering the pages of questions. He returned the completed journal to Lindsay a year later. He finished the journal by writing a note to the girls on the extra blank pages.

Lindsay and Kelsey,

I've been through a lot in my life. Some good and some bad. You learn a lot as you are growing up and you will make some mistakes. My prayer for the two of you is that you put your faith, love, and trust in the Lord Jesus Christ and pray and follow what he has in mind for you as you become young adults. I've asked the Lord so often to watch over you, and one day I won't be here any longer to help with that. I thank God for both of you every day and Lord willing, I'll be around for a while to watch you grow in Christ. Let our Lord Jesus Christ guide you through every day, and I hope you'll always love me as much as I love you!

Always! Dad

Jack didn't live long enough to see God answer his prayers for Lindsay and Kelsey's salvation. Cirrhosis and liver cancer, remnants of his former alcoholism, cut his life short. He died three years after returning the journal. Jack gave his two daughters another gift. On his deathbed, he called them to his side, handed Lindsay his Bible and said, "Please take this. I want you and Kelsey to read it."

In the months and years after her father's passing, Lindsay missed her dad. The journal he completed for her and her sister became a precious treasure, which she regularly turned to for comfort. It felt like she was spending time with him as she sat on her bed reading his answers to the many questions. As she read and reread the journal, she noticed that her dad kept talking about Jesus. She remembered the Bible he gave them and began to read it too. Reading his Bible cultivated an increasing hunger in her to know God like her dad knew God.

Eventually, the Spirit of God convicted Lindsay. She realized that she had to turn from her sin and live for Jesus. The day she decided to repent and trust Jesus, she felt a burden lift from her shoulders. Something had changed. Suddenly the pages of the journal sprang to life. Lindsay, recalling that moment shared, "I remember reading the pages in the journal after God saved me thinking—'Oh my goodness, I can't believe this. I'm feeling what Dad felt. Now I know what it feels like to know Jesus!'"

From that point on, Lindsay began to pray that God would save Kelsey and allow her to enjoy the freedom and joy she experienced. Kelsey was tangled in an unhealthy relationship with a guy and had pulled away from the family over the previous few years. So the phone call that came the night Lindsay prayed with Destin, Maria, and Emma was a miracle.

When Lindsay picked up Kelsey the next morning, Kelsey agreed to attend the breakfast at the church. Then she decided to stay for the message and discussion that followed. She was assigned to a small group that Destin and Lindsay helped lead. The breakfast and discussion seemed to go well, but when Lindsay asked Kelsey how she thought it went, Kelsey responded, "I probably won't come back." But inside God was working. She had enjoyed the message, which began to sink in over the following days. Kelsey's life was a mess and she felt broken. Though she lived an hour away and had to close her restaurant the night before the next Bridge meeting, she still was at the church when Lindsay arrived the next week. When Lindsay saw her sister's car, she began to rejoice.

A few weeks later, God began to close the deal on bringing Kelsey into his kingdom. One Bridge Course morning, Kelsey awoke with a start from a dream in which she was in a dark room, then turned a corner and saw Jesus hanging on the cross, crying out in agony. The message that day was on the crucifixion. It deeply affected Kelsey. She knew that the dream and the message came from God. "He wanted me to know it was real," she recalled. Finally, at week seven, Jack's prayers were answered as his second daughter called out to Jesus to forgive her sins. At that moment, like her sister, she felt a weight lift from her shoulders and knew that God had come into her life.

Immediately Kelsey's life began to change. She stopped drinking and smoking and started living for the Lord. Her boyfriend broke up with her, leaving her homeless, but her grandmother welcomed her into her home. Kelsey finished the Bridge Course, became a member of the church, and now prays for others who still need Jesus. While Jack's prayers for his daughters were not answered in his lifetime, they were answered nonetheless. Jesus said that there is great rejoicing in heaven whenever a sinner repents (Luke 15:7). Jack was present with Jesus in heaven when the Lord announced each daughter's salvation. We can be sure that no one cheered louder.

One of the questions in the journal Lindsay gave her father was, "What spiritual legacy would you like to leave for others?"

Jack answered, "It comes from the Bible, James 1:12. 'Blessed is the man who perseveres under trial, because when he has stood the test, he will receive the crown of life that God has promised to those who love him'" (NIV). Lindsay and Kelsey are the two largest jewels that adorn Jack's crown. Today his daughters treasure the journal he wrote and long for the day when they are united with their dad and can thank him face to face.

CHAPTER 15

Your Kids
and a Plague of Locusts

Exodus 10:1–15

Introduction to the Week

Five hundred years ago, Michelangelo completed his magnificent sculpture of Moses, meant to adorn the tomb of Pope Julius II. The deliverer of Israel is seated on a throne, the long locks of his beard flowing down into the folds of his robe from a strong jaw. Captivated by this stately image, Cecil B. DeMille cast Charlton Heston to play the role of Moses in his epic film, *The Ten Commandments*, because of Heston's striking resemblance to Michelangelo's Moses.

The movie cost thirteen million dollars to shoot, the most expensive film ever back in 1956. Paramount's investment paid off handsomely. *The Ten Commandments* grossed over fifty-six million dollars in its first year—and that was when you could purchase a ticket for fifty cents! The film featured fourteen thousand extras and fifteen thousand live animals. Parts of the film were shot in Egypt, and the special effects of the movie set a new standard for filmmaking (and were later used by Steven Spielberg).

DeMille recognized the incredible value of the exodus story. While some of the subplots were fictionalized to fill in the story line, DeMille purposed to keep the script faithful to the biblical text and historical accounts of Moses's life from Philo and Josephus. Prior to the opening credits, DeMille recorded a personal introduction to the movie, when he came out from behind a curtain to explain the importance of the film. DeMille said, "Our intention was not to create a story, but to be worthy of the divinely-inspired story created three thousand years ago."

This week we'll look back at a portion of the amazing exodus story, the plague of locusts. If you are wondering, *What has the plague of grasshoppers got to do with parenting?*, you may be surprised to know that this epic story of slavery and suffering, persecution and plagues, and death and deliverance unfolded just as God planned and purposed for the sake of our children.

Day One

God Wrote the Story for Our Kids

> Then the LORD said to Moses, "Go in to Pharaoh, for I have hardened his heart and the heart of his servants, that I may show these signs of mine among them, and that you may tell in the hearing of your son and of your grandson how I have dealt harshly with the Egyptians and what signs I have done among them, that you may know that I am the LORD."
>
> So Moses and Aaron went in to Pharaoh and said to him, "Thus says the LORD, the God of the Hebrews, 'How long will you refuse to humble yourself before me? Let my people go, that they may serve me. For if you refuse to let my people

go, behold, tomorrow I will bring locusts into your country, and they shall cover the face of the land, so that no one can see the land. And they shall eat what is left to you after the hail, and they shall eat every tree of yours that grows in the field, and they shall fill your houses and the houses of all your servants and of all the Egyptians, as neither your fathers nor your grandfathers have seen, from the day they came on earth to this day.'" Then he turned and went out from Pharaoh. (Exodus 10:1–6)

Ponder Anew

By the time we come to chapter 10 of the exodus story, God has heard the cry of his people to deliver them from their slavery in Egypt. God's great drama of rescue has begun. God turned the Nile River to blood and plagued the Egyptians with frogs, flies, gnats, death to livestock, boils and hail, but still, Pharaoh refused to let the people of Israel go. As each plague comes, Pharaoh relents, but then, once the threat subsides, he hardens his heart and again refuses to release God's people.

The obvious question arising from this story is, Why doesn't God just wipe out Pharaoh? When the Assyrians encamped against Jerusalem, the angel of the Lord visited the camp of the Assyrians and struck down 185,000 men. Why all the drama of frogs and flies, blood and boils? We get the answer from God in this chapter, just before the ninth plague. God is writing a story for our children so that they will know the awesome power of God and put their faith in him. Look again at what he tells Moses:

". . . for I have hardened his heart and the heart of his servants, that I may show these signs of mine among them, and that you may tell in the hearing of your son and of your grandson how I have dealt harshly with the Egyptians and what signs I have done among them, that you may know that I am the LORD." (Exodus 10:1–2)

While Pharaoh hardened his own heart (Exodus 8:15, 32), God was also hardening his heart and the hearts of his servants as a judgment for their evil, all in accord with his master plan. God was not forcing Pharaoh to sin; Pharaoh rebelled against God willingly and deserved the punishment he received for his rebellion. Still, God's absolute sovereignty reigns over all, so that even evil is under his authority and accomplishes his purpose. Here, God uses the evil, stubborn rebellion of Pharaoh to create a story so spectacular that, all by itself, it has the power to save.

The Exodus plagues, culminating in the plague of death, provide the clearest foreshadowing of the gospel in all the Old Testament. Therefore, God decreed that the story must not be forgotten. In giving the instructions for the Passover, God instructed Moses that the Passover meal was to commemorate the unfolding of the exodus drama for all time (Exodus 12:23–27).

The Passover tradition continued until the evening of the Last Supper, when Jesus revealed the true meaning of the age-old tradition and instituted a new memorial. So today, rather than look back to remember the blood of the lamb slain, daubed on the doorframes of the Israelites, we remember Jesus sacrificed for our sins.

What an incredible thing to consider that God, looking down through the corridor of time, saw your son—Bob, David, Jayden, Caleb—and your daughter—Elizabeth, Hailey, Jordan, and Susan. For their sake, he created the story of the exodus, which pointed to the greatest story ever told, the gospel story. The meaning of the Hebrew phrase from Exodus 10:2, "that you may tell in the hearing of your son and of your grandson," extends beyond the second-generation grandchildren to all future offspring, the generations of grandchildren to come. That includes our children.

As parents hungry to see our children drawn into the kingdom, we can at least ensure that our kids know the story. For it is this age-old gospel story that God intends to provoke their questions. We share the story and then trust the Holy Spirit to stir their hearts and affections with the story we've told them. Here is what we must believe: that God knew and considered each of our children as he slowly unfolded the ten plagues. God saw our sons and daughters when he gave up his only Son for us and our kids. When we think back to Jesus hanging on the cross for the forgiveness of sins for all who believe, we must trust that he saw our sons and daughters and will draw them to himself. The gospel story is life, and our hope for the salvation of our children—and what a glorious hope it is!

Bring It Home

- What does the plague of locusts have to do with our children?
- Read Exodus 3:7–10. How can God's hearing of Israel's cries for deliverance encourage us to continue praying for our children?

Day Two

The Enemy Is After Our Children

> Then Pharaoh's servants said to him, "How long shall this man be a snare to us? Let the men go, that they may serve the Lord their God. Do you not yet understand that Egypt is ruined?" So Moses and Aaron were brought back to Pharaoh. And he said

to them, "Go, serve the LORD your God. But which ones are to go?" Moses said, "We will go with our young and our old. We will go with our sons and daughters and with our flocks and herds, for we must hold a feast to the LORD." But he said to them, "The LORD be with you, if ever I let you and your little ones go! Look, you have some evil purpose in mind. No! Go, the men among you, and serve the LORD, for that is what you are asking." And they were driven out from Pharaoh's presence. (Exodus 10:7–11)

Ponder Anew

The Enemy knows that his best attack against the gospel is to wipe out the faith of our children and the passing of our faith to the next generation. And so, while God has ensured that the gospel will be carried on through his Word, the Enemy was working to thwart God's plan. He is still active today against our children. We see his scheming in the stubbornness of Pharaoh not to let the children go.

As we read the exodus story, we see that by the time we reach Exodus 10 and the hail has destroyed the crops in Exodus 9, the servants of Pharaoh have seen enough. They know that Egypt is ruined. The plagues have brought untold suffering upon Egypt. The loss of livestock and crops to that point already ensure that Egypt would suffer greatly. They recommend that Pharaoh let the Israelites go. But Pharaoh is not ready to relent. He rejects his counselors' advice and calls Moses back into his chambers and offers a cunning plan. He will allow everyone but the children to go. The response Moses gives should inform our response as we face attacks upon our children: "We will go with our young and our old. We will go with our sons and daughters." Like Moses, we must declare, "We will not leave our children behind!"

When God finished with Pharaoh, Moses and the people of God left Egypt for a land of promise, flowing with milk and honey, a land where God would be the God of Israel, and they would be his people. Looking back through a gospel lens, we see that the Promised Land is a foreshadowing of heaven. Like Moses, we must insist before our Enemy that we will not go without our children.

We are on that same journey—to the Promised Land. Jesus said, "Let not your hearts be troubled. Believe in God; believe also in me. In my Father's house are many rooms. If it were not so, would I have told you that I go to prepare a place for you? And if I go and prepare a place for you, I will come again and will take you to myself, that where I am you may be also" (John 14:1–3).

Remember what Peter said in his letter? "Blessed be the God and Father of our Lord Jesus Christ! According to his great mercy, he has caused us to be born again to a living hope through the resurrection of Jesus Christ from the dead, to an inheritance that is imperishable, undefiled, and unfading, kept in heaven for you, who by God's power are being guarded through faith for a salvation ready to be revealed in the last time" (1 Peter 1:3–5).

In the face of the temptations thrown at us by our Enemy, and amid our children's struggles with their own sinful flesh, we must refuse to give up on any of them. Instead, we stand with Moses and call out for help to our God, who directs all history in conformity to his purpose, even the evil that looks to undermine his glorious plan. Then, before our Enemy, we voice our agreement with Moses through our trust in God: We will not go without our children.

Bring It Home

- Write out a prayer that declares, before God and all the forces of evil, your renewed commitment to insist that all your children go with you to the Promised Land. Ask God to deliver them from Egypt, a picture of the wicked bondage of sin and the flesh. Pray this prayer the rest of the week.

- How does John 6:37–39 continue the theme that God will not leave behind a single one of his children?

Day Three

The Story Points to Christ

"This day shall be for you a memorial day, and you shall keep it as a feast to the LORD; throughout your generations, as a statute forever, you shall keep it as a feast. Seven days you shall eat unleavened bread. On the first day you shall remove leaven out of your houses, for if anyone eats what is leavened, from the first day until the seventh day, that person shall be cut off from Israel. On the first day you shall hold a holy assembly, and on the seventh day a holy assembly. No work shall be done on those days. But what everyone needs to eat, that alone may be prepared by you. And you shall observe the Feast of Unleavened Bread, for on this very day I brought your hosts out of the land of Egypt. Therefore you shall observe this day, throughout your generations, as a statute forever. In the first month, from the fourteenth day of the month at evening, you shall eat unleavened bread until the twenty-first day of the month at evening. For seven days no leaven is to be found in your houses. If anyone eats what is leavened, that person will be cut off from the congregation of Israel, whether he is a sojourner or a native of the land.

You shall eat nothing leavened; in all your dwelling places you shall eat unleavened bread."

Then Moses called all the elders of Israel and said to them, "Go and select lambs for yourselves according to your clans, and kill the Passover lamb. Take a bunch of hyssop and dip it in the blood that is in the basin, and touch the lintel and the two doorposts with the blood that is in the basin. None of you shall go out of the door of his house until the morning. For the LORD will pass through to strike the Egyptians, and when he sees the blood on the lintel and on the two doorposts, the LORD will pass over the door and will not allow the destroyer to enter your houses to strike you. You shall observe this rite as a statute for you and for your sons forever. And when you come to the land that the LORD will give you, as he has promised, you shall keep this service. And when your children say to you, 'What do you mean by this service?' you shall say, 'It is the sacrifice of the LORD's Passover, for he passed over the houses of the people of Israel in Egypt, when he struck the Egyptians but spared our houses.'" And the people bowed their heads and worshiped. (Exodus 12:14–27)

Ponder Anew

"And when your children say to you, 'What do you mean by this service?'" Notice that it does not say, "And *if* your children say to you . . ." God has created such a magnificent memorial that it will provoke the curiosity of our children. While not all Christian families celebrate the traditional Jewish Passover meal, all believers are commanded to celebrate the Lord's Supper, which fills the Passover with its true meaning. God was doing more than delivering Israel out of the hand of

Egypt; God was painting the larger picture of his great gospel deliverance.

God's deliverance of his people from slavery in Egypt was a picture of our deeper struggle as slaves to sin. Jesus said, "I say to you, everyone who practices sin is a slave to sin" (John 8:34). This struggle goes on in all our lives, but God continues his great deliverance. With the sacrifice of his Son, the true Passover Lamb of God (1 Corinthians 5:7; John 1:29) who takes away the sins of the world, no further sacrifice for sin is needed.

Again and again, when the people of God sinned and experienced his judgment, God sent prophets to remind them of the exodus. Their exhortations contained a future promise— that God would continue to deliver his people and one day that deliverance would be complete. Today, we know that the deliverance from sin is complete through Jesus, who will one day return to lead his people home to our true Promised Land. Let us not fear that we will need to leave our children behind. As we struggle against the Enemy and the bondage of sin, let us stand with Moses and insist that we will not go without our children!

Not a single child of Israel was left behind in Egypt, and it was those children who possessed the land. When God gave the prophet Haggai a word of encouragement to share with the people, he foretold our final deliverance. Let the words God designed to encourage Israel to rebuild the temple encourage us:

> "Be strong, all you people of the land, declares the LORD. Work, for I am with you, declares the LORD of hosts, according to the covenant that I made with you when you came out of Egypt. My Spirit remains in your midst. Fear not. For thus says the LORD of hosts: Yet once more, in a little while, I will shake the heavens and the earth and the sea and the dry land. And I will shake all nations, so that the

treasures of all nations shall come in, and I will fill this house with glory, says the LORD of hosts. The silver is mine, and the gold is mine, declares the LORD of hosts. The latter glory of this house shall be greater than the former, says the LORD of hosts. And in this place I will give peace, declares the LORD of hosts." (Haggai 2:4–9)

Jesus said, "Destroy this temple, and in three days I will raise it up" (John 2:19). We know that he was referring to his body and he did, in fact, rise from the dead on the third day. The latter glory is so far greater than the former! Then, the glory of the Lord filled a building of stone; today the same presence of God fills our hearts.

He is still at work, delivering his people from Egypt. Let us have faith that he will not leave a single son or daughter behind and let us trust that the great gospel story itself can be used of God to save our children, that they too will be filled with the glorious presence of the Lord.

Bring It Home

- How can knowing God's commitment to deliver his people encourage your faith regarding your children?
- Look up the following Scriptures: John 3:16; Isaiah 44:3–5; Isaiah 54:13–14; Acts 16:31.
- How do these passages point to God's commitment to save every one of his children?

Real Life

I can remember holding my newborn daughter Emma in my arms, comforting her late-night crying and wondering about her future. Who would she grow up to be? How would God save her? Whom would she marry? As I sang lullabies to comfort her crying, I prayed God would rescue her from sin and guide her. God answered my prayers. Emma grew up to be a fine, godly, respectful daughter. God drew her to himself in her early high school years. She studied elementary education and pursued a missional teaching position in the impoverished inner city, which wasn't a part of my comfortably fabricated future for her.

As for marriage, well, let's say God wasn't following my comfortable script for that either. I'll never forget the day Emma pulled Lois and me aside in the kitchen to talk. She and Martha had reached out to Destin after he returned home to recover from his gunshot wound. Each Sunday night they, along with my son Noah, hung out around a bonfire with a group of older teens and college students to worship, pray, and fellowship. It was there that Emma noticed God touching Destin's life.

After pulling us aside, Emma said, "I believe God wants me to pray for Destin because he is going to become my husband. What is up with that?" She went on to explain her concerns given his addictive past, his need to be established in a career, and the fact that it would be years before he would be able to marry. She was torn. She could see God at work in his life, but the obstacles to a future together weighed on the other side of the balance scale like a cinderblock.

My mind raced as she spoke. Only a few weeks earlier, Destin had scheduled a pastoral appointment to meet with me. Even though I had cared for his family for many years, I was aware that twenty-something guys didn't schedule appointments with me unless they were interested in one of my daughters—which he was. Destin began our meeting by confessing his sin and bringing me up-to-date on his failures. He wouldn't be ready to pursue a wife until he was clean for a year, he explained. Destin needed to pay off his mountain of fines, get a job, and establish a career so that he could provide before he would be ready to marry. But, he added, he was interested in my daughter.

I didn't dare let on to Emma or Lois anything about the earlier conversation. I just listened and prayed for wisdom. I agreed with Emma that Destin was in no place to pursue a relationship, but for now she should at least follow the impression to pray for him. Inside, God began working on my heart and impressed the question upon me: *Do you believe in redemption?* For years, I counseled Destin's mother, Maria, encouraging her that God could save her son and deliver him from drugs. Now that it was happening, was I willing to allow God to use my daughter as a part of his restoration plan?

As the months unfolded, Destin continued pressing into God and reaching others caught in the prison of drug addiction. The bonfire crowd prayed fervently for their friends, and young men and women were getting saved. They started sitting in the front row of our church on Sunday, lifting their hands, praising God for his deliverance, with my daughter Emma smack in the middle of them.

Destin, who had always had an incredible work ethic, took a job with his uncle installing garage doors. He soon ran installations without supervision. He began paying off all his debts, stayed clean and, most importantly, demonstrated a passion for God that affected everyone around him. Six months later he was back in my office to give me an update and share his desire to pursue my daughter Emma.

I reminded him of the wisdom of waiting a year, but inside I was concerned that this wouldn't be nearly enough time. I could not deny God's work in Destin's life, but I found it difficult to add my daughter into the equation of God's redemption. In the meantime, Emma grew in her affection for Destin as she prayed for him. We directed her to seek God further and helped her count the costs of pursuing a relationship with a man with his past.

A year from our first November meeting, Destin's name appeared in my pastoral schedule again. I knew he had remained drug-free and paid off his debt. He continued to minister to others who were now getting baptized and joining our church. The fruit of God's grace on Destin's life was evident for all to see. In that meeting, Destin asked for permission to pursue my daughter. I agreed.

A few weeks later, Emma shared with Destin the prayer journal entry she had written years before, when she began to pray for her future husband's salvation. Destin was amazed to discover that the very week she started her journal was the same week he knelt in his prison cell and gave his life to Christ, after a phone call with his mom.

Within a few months, Destin was back in my office, asking to marry my daughter. Things were going far too fast for my comfort. He explained that he believed God was bringing the two of them together and referenced the timing of Emma's journal and his salvation.

Then Destin pulled out a piece of paper and began to read a list of vows—but not vows he planned to vow to Emma. This was a list of vows to me, her father. As he read each one carefully and looked into my eyes, vowing to care for my daughter, the Spirit of God filled my heart. As he spoke, I could not deny the miracle God had accomplished in his life. Destin explained that he paid off his fines and debt, and established a career, excelling at his work. And, to my shock, he already had a ring.

He stuck his hand in his pocket and pulled out a diamond engagement ring of inestimable value, for it was the ring his father had given his mother, Maria. I knew the moment I saw the ring that God was doing a miracle before my eyes. Then Destin read to me the letter his mother had presented with the ring.

Dear Destin,

I am full of joy with the work the Father has done and is doing in your life, and I am so pleased with how you have chosen Emma, a beautiful, godly woman, to be by your side and walk through life and ministry with.

This ring is a symbol of eighteen years of faithful marriage between me and your dad. Your father was a man of faith who loved God first, then his wife with all his heart. He cared for, protected, and provided for his family with vigilance. This ring reminds me of his steadfast love for me, as Christ loved the church. I trust that you will be the same for Emma.

Consider this ring, the ring that your dad pledged his love to me, as "the crown with which his mother crowned him on the day of his wedding, on the day of the gladness of his heart" (Song of Songs 3:11).

I am rejoicing with you as I know your father is too, and I pass down this ring to you with all my love and blessing. Mom

At that moment, I had a choice to make. Did I truly believe in God's deliverance? That question swirled in my mind, quickly followed by the answer I gave Destin as he asked for my daughter's hand. "Yes," I told him.

While the Enemy means to imprison our children in bondage to sin, God is about writing a story of deliverance. He hears our prayers and calls for mercy, and we must not give up praying, knowing that he can deliver our children and weave them into his grand tapestry of grace. We will celebrate the testimony of his grace for all time and eternity as we each, in turn, share story after story of God's redeeming work.

Lois and I met at Maria's house after the engagement to celebrate. Maria smiled as we considered all that God had done. It was truly remarkable. Reflecting on the many years I had encouraged her to stay the course and trust God and his redemption, Maria said, "Who would have known or believed that your daughter Emma was a part of the plan?!"

CHAPTER 16

He Will Direct Your Paths

Proverbs 3:1–8

Introduction to the Week

In May of 1850, Hungarian obstetrician Ignaz Semmelweiss approached the podium of the Vienna Medical Societies lecture hall to deliver a lifesaving message to his colleagues. It could be summed up in three words: "Wash your hands." In those days, it was standard practice for doctors to perform autopsies in the morning and then examine expectant mothers without washing their hands. This resulted in a far higher rate of death for doctor-examined patients than those cared for by midwives. For three years prior to his address, Semmelweiss directed his medical students to wash their hands in chlorinated lime solution before examining expectant mothers or delivering babies. Now he wanted his colleagues to do the same. But many of the other doctors were outraged at the accusation that their lack of handwashing could result in death. They would rather lean on their own understanding and their traditional medical practice.

Around the same time that Semmelweiss was trying to convince his fellow obstetricians to wash their hands, Joseph Lister observed that patients treated for compound fractures often died from infections, while those with simple breaks nearly always survived. Lister reasoned that surgeons were introducing the infections to the patients. In keeping with this theory, Lister began washing his hands and wearing clean clothes with some improvements in patient outcomes. Like Semmelweiss's colleagues in Vienna, many of Lister's fellow surgeons scoffed at his ideas. They believed blood-splattered clothing was the mark of an accomplished surgeon. In 1867, after reading a study published by Louis Pasteur, who was also ridiculed for his germ theory, Lister had begun washing his hands and instruments in carbolic acid with great success. Later he published his findings, but many doctors disregarded the truth he presented. They too would rather trust in their own understanding, saying they would not believe in something they could not see.

People, in general, have a tough time trusting in what they cannot see, taste, or touch. King Solomon knew that this materialistic tendency affected a person's ability to trust God in challenging times. While Proverbs 3:5, "Do not lean on your own understanding," is one of the most quoted verses in the Bible, it is often one of the most difficult to follow. This week we will take a closer look at Proverbs 3 to help us learn to trust the Lord with all our hearts.

Day One

Our God Can Deliver Us

> My son, do not forget my teaching, but let your heart keep my commandments, for length of days and years of life and peace they will add to you. (Proverbs 3:1–2)

Ponder Anew

Solomon's words echo the promise God laid out in the fifth commandment: Honor your father and mother that it might go well with you and bring you long life. While these early Proverbs chapters capture the advice a father holds out for his son, the truths Solomon shared apply to all God's children, parents included.

When we trust God's commandments enough to keep them, we are entrusting our lives to the God who created the commands. The word "commandments" generally refer to all of God's commands in Scripture but more specifically refers to the Ten Commandments that God gave Moses on the mountain, engraved upon stone tablets. If we look back at the day God first spoke those commands, we find that the context is God's magnificent deliverance of Israel from slavery in Egypt. This is how the commandments begin:

> And God spoke all these words, saying, "I am the Lord your God, who brought you out of the land of Egypt, out of the house of slavery.
> "You shall have no other gods before me.
> "You shall not make for yourself a carved image, or any likeness of anything that is in heaven above, or that is in the earth beneath, or that is in the water under the earth. You shall not bow down to them or serve them, for I the Lord your God am a jealous God, visiting the iniquity of the fathers on the children to the third and the fourth generation of those who hate me, but showing steadfast love to thousands of those who love me and keep my commandments." (Exodus 20:1–6)

The very first thing God says is, I am the one who "brought you out of the land of Egypt." The implication is clear: If God could deliver Israel out of Egypt so powerfully, then we can trust that his commands will result in our deliverance. As he did with Israel, he hears our cries for help and will answer us. It seems crazy to think that anyone who knew what God had done would turn from him to a mute idol or doubt his capacity to save.

But that, in fact, is what Israel did. They turned from the God who delivered them and fell into complaining and, eventually, idolatry. That is the same thing we do in the midst of our trials when we complain against God instead of running to him for help. When we turn from God, we end up serving idols just like Israel. That is what we do when we trust in our own strength to solve our problem or, worse, give up and turn to alcohol or eating or pornography to soothe our souls. Idolatry and rejecting God's commands are at the heart of our complaining, bitterness, and (for those who do not repent) falling away from faith and giving up all hope.

So where do we find our peace? We find it in believing that the God who delivered Israel can deliver us. He is with us, just as he was with Israel in the pillar of cloud when they were pushed up against the Red Sea; just as he was present in the boat with the disciples in the midst of the storm, ready to rebuke the wind and the waves (Mark 4:35–39). Back then, the disciples were still learning that Jesus was the same God who had delivered Israel from the Egyptians. Today, we know who Jesus is, and we know the Spirit of God, who is always with us to deliver us. We can trust him to keep us safe.

When trapped against the Red Sea, Israel panicked despite the fact that God's presence went before them in a pillar of cloud. Though Jesus lay asleep in their boat, the disciples also shook with fear. It was not until they were safely through the Red Sea that Israel rejoiced, and not until the storm was calmed that the disciples praised the Lord. But the peace promised by Solomon does not require our storms be calmed. Jesus rebuked the disciples for fearing the storm at all. He said to them, "Why are you so afraid? Have you still no faith?" (Mark 4:40). The point of his correction was that if Jesus is in the boat, you need not worry. You can find peace in the midst of your storm.

God's commandments remind us that he is the Sovereign Lord who commands all things. In him we can place our trust. For if he could deliver Israel out of the hand of Pharaoh, he can deliver us. Our trust is safe when placed solely in him.

Bring It Home

- Have you found yourself complaining to God that he hasn't delivered you instead of continuing to ask for his deliverance?
- How confident are you that, if you were to follow God's commands, you would find peace in the midst of your storm? How is this an accurate indication of your level of faith in God?

Day Two

Steadfast Love

Let not steadfast love and faithfulness forsake you; bind them around your neck; write them on the tablet of your heart. So you will find favor and good success in the sight of God and man. (Proverbs 3:3–4)

Ponder Anew

In today's verses, Solomon connects memorizing God's commands (writing them on the tablet of your heart) with knowing and experiencing God's steadfast love. This too is a reference to the opening of God's commandments, where

Moses tells us that God reveals his "steadfast love to thousands of those who love me and keep my commandments" (Exodus 20:6). Memorizing Scripture is one of the best ways to stay grounded in the Word in the midst of a trial.

Consider how writing the following verses "on the tablet of your heart" can build your faith for your parenting trial.

> The LORD is a stronghold for the oppressed, a stronghold in times of trouble. And those who know your name put their trust in you, for you, O LORD, have not forsaken those who seek you. (Psalm 9:9–10)

> When the righteous cry for help, the LORD hears and delivers them out of all their troubles. The LORD is near to the brokenhearted and saves the crushed in spirit. (Psalm 34:17–18)

> Fear not, for I am with you; be not dismayed, for I am your God; I will strengthen you, I will help you, I will uphold you with my righteous right hand. (Isaiah 41:10)

> I know, O LORD, that your rules are righteous, and that in faithfulness you have afflicted me. Let your steadfast love comfort me according to your promise to your servant. (Psalm 119:75–76)

The word "steadfast" appears in the ESV Bible 219 times. In 194 of those cases, the word "love" follows the word "steadfast." God's love toward us is steadfast. Our trials do not overtax it and our sin doesn't neutralize it. About the only way for God's steadfast love to fail us is if we ignore it. So let us not forsake God's commandments. Instead, let's write them on the tablet of our hearts, knowing that they have the power to encourage us and bring us peace.

Bring It Home

- Which of the four suggested verses most encourages you? Take time to memorize it over the next few days. Once you have committed it to memory, share it with at least one other person.
- Do a word search on the "steadfast love" of God. (You can do this through a Bible program or by searching the internet for "Bible verses about the steadfast love of God.") See if you can find a second verse to commit to memory.

Day Three

Refreshed Down to the Bone

> Trust in the LORD with all your heart, and do not lean on your own understanding. In all your ways acknowledge him, and he will make straight your paths. Be not wise in your own eyes; fear the LORD, and turn away from evil. It will be healing to your flesh and refreshment to your bones. (Proverbs 3:5–8)

Ponder Anew

Through the earlier verses in this passage, we learned to look for our peace not in the ending of our storm, but in trusting God and his Word in the midst of it. We also learned that when we write God's commands on the tablet of our heart, we can better apply them to our lives. We can now consider verses 5–8 in their broader context.

Solomon contrasts trusting the Lord (which we've learned involves trusting his commandments) with trusting in our own understanding (what we think apart from God's Word).

He then exhorts us to abandon our own understanding to trust the Lord "with all our heart." There is no halfway here—but trust is like that. We are either trusting in the Lord or we are not. If you find yourself wanting to trust God but weak in faith, cry out to God to help you fully trust him, like the boy's father who called out to Jesus to help him overcome his unbelief (Mark 9:24).

The promise Solomon offers those who trust the Lord is that God will make their path straight. The straight path in Scripture is set in contrast to the crooked path that turns away from God's commandments. So the promise is that, if we trust in the Lord with all our heart and keep his commandments, God will help us stay on the righteous path, turning from evil to follow his Word. There is no greater hope in trial.

What is the outcome of remaining on the path that does not turn from the Lord? The promised result is a healing and refreshment that we know down deep in our bones. Only one thing can bring that depth of refreshment: fellowship with God himself amid life's storms.

If you need some refreshing in the midst of your parenting storm, write another verse upon the tablet of your heart and then trust and pray those verses. Believe that God will make your path straight and bring refreshment to your soul.

Bring It Home

- Proverbs 3:5 begins with the phrase, "Trust in the Lord." What does trusting the Lord mean practically?
- Can you remember a time when you put your trust in the Lord and found peace in the midst of a storm? Remembering what God has done in the past is one of the most effective ways to trust God in the present. Like the Israelites, we too often forget our past deliverance amid present storms.

- Make a list of the past times that you trusted God in a trial and found peace. Then reflect on the unchangeable nature of God. He is the same God today, who still offers his steadfast love and peace for our present trials.

Real Life

The day before Destin and Emma were to be married, Destin posted a prayer of praise, thanking God for providing him the woman of his dreams, and asking God to bless the next day's wedding. Destin wrote, "I pray that we would witness the glory of Yahweh Almighty tomorrow, that his love will be magnified for all to see, that this picture of marriage would reflect Jesus's perfect love for his people." Knowing that the forecast called for severe thunderstorms, with the reception scheduled to be held under a tent, Destin concluded his post by praying, "I pray in SO much faith that he would hold the rain until 5 p.m. That we would look on this prayer and all might say, 'He heard us!' And it would glory your name all the more!" While the storm threatened to ruin the outdoor reception, Destin knew that the God who was with him in the boat of life was able to calm the storm.

The next morning, I watched the weather forecast intently. It continued to forecast severe thunderstorms with damaging winds. The building manager for the church needed a decision on where to set up the tables and chairs—under the tent or in the church lobby? I spoke to Destin on the phone. His trust in the Lord stirred me. "I'm believing God is going to hold back the rain," he said with confidence. Personally, I wasn't so sure. I tended to lean more on my own understanding. If it had been up to me, I would have moved the reception inside, but hearing Destin's strong faith in God inspired me. We passed the word to the facilities manager. "We'll do the reception outside. We're trusting God to hold back the storms."

While we were discussing the weather, I opened the church doors for the ladies to do their hair and put on their gowns. A few hours later, they left the church to join the groomsmen and take pictures at a local state park. Minutes after they left, I received a scary call. My two daughters, Emma and Martha, the bride and maid of honor, were involved in a serious auto accident. A car driving in the passing lane suddenly decided to make a right-hand turn, across their lane, into a side street. The car turned sharply, directly in front of my daughters, whose car was traveling at 45 miles per hour. As the cars collided and began to spin, broken bits of car parts scattered for fifty feet in all directions. Emma remembers closing her eyes and, when the spinning stopped, she wondered if her hands had broken off, so fierce had been the impact. Once she realized her hands were okay, her next thought was to see how much blood there was on her dress and the floor below. To her amazement, there was none.

"Dad, we were in a serious accident but we are okay. What should we do?" That was the message as I raced to the scene of the accident. Two of the others involved were taken by ambulance to a local hospital with non-life threatening injuries. My daughters were shaken up and bruised with seatbelt burns, but were not seriously injured. The wedding would go on! I drove them to the state park, where Destin and the groomsmen were gathered in a circle, praying.

Earlier, when leaving the church, Emma had asked Martha if it would be okay to travel the short distance without her seatbelt to keep her dress from wrinkling. Martha insisted that she wear the seatbelt, wrinkles or no wrinkles. On a day when the bride's wishes are to be honored, God saw fit to put her in the capable hands of a loving sister who also happens to be a registered nurse and has seen her fair share of trauma.

As for the weather, the thunderstorms came nowhere near us, as though God wanted to bless the faith of one young groom who wanted to give God the glory. I danced the father-daughter dance on the cobblestone walkway under blue skies with puffy white clouds. Destin trusted in the Lord with all his heart for that day, and God made his path straight. He asked that we would witness the glory of Yahweh during the wedding—and that we did.

CHAPTER 17

Keep Your Eyes on Jesus

Hebrews 12:1–15

Introduction to the Week

"Keep your eyes on number 26." The coach's words rang in Abebe's head as he tied the laces of the uncomfortable shoes handed to him for running the 1960 Olympics in Rome. Abebe Bikila didn't own a pair of running shoes. He ran barefoot back in Ethiopia, often across rough, rocky terrain. Abebe, a soldier in the Imperial Guard, wasn't a part of his country's Olympic team until Ethiopia's star runner, Wami Biratu, dropped out of the games due to illness. Abebe took his place. He had won several marathons in Ethiopia but wasn't used to running in shoes. He pondered his coach's counsel to look for number 26. Moroccan runner Rhadi Ben Abdesselam would be wearing that number. If he could keep up with Rhadi, he'd have a chance to win. After a few uncomfortable practice miles, Abebe took the shoes off and decided to run without them. He wanted the world to know that his country, Ethiopia, won with "determination and heroism."[1] He didn't need the help of the fancy shoes.

---

1. https://www.olympic.org/news/barefooted-bikila-steps-in-for-heroic-marathon-triumph

As the field of runners gathered at the start line, Abebe searched for number 26 in vain. Unbeknownst to Abebe, Rhadi, the Moroccan runner, could not find the bib with number 26 and had to resort to using a bib with the number 185. So, since he failed to find number 26, Abebe instead set his eyes on the road ahead and the finish line. Little did he realize that he ran neck and neck with Rhadi all the way. When at last the finish line came in sight, Abebe kicked into high gear and sprinted to the finish to win the race and break the Olympic record. The next day the papers reported that "it had taken Italy a million-man army to defeat Ethiopia, but only one lone Ethiopian soldier to conquer Rome,"[2] and he did it barefoot!

Four years later, despite recovering from an appendectomy weeks before the race, Abebe took his second gold medal in the Tokyo Olympics. He broke his own record, finishing four minutes ahead of the closest runner. With no runners to chase, once again Abebe kept his eyes on the finish line.

Tragedy struck in 1969. An auto accident left Abebe paralyzed from the waist down. Confined to a wheelchair, Abebe took up archery to compete in paraplegic sports. When asked about his accident in a later interview, Abebe said, "It was the will of God that I won the Olympics, and it was the will of God that I met with my accident, I accepted those victories as I accept this tragedy."[3]

The writer of the book of Hebrews compared life to running a race where we must keep our eyes focused on Jesus. Christ is our prize at the finish line; keeping our focus on him can help us win the race set before us.

2. David Maraniss, *Rome 1960: The Olympics that Changed the World* (New York: Simon & Schuster; Reprint edition, July 14, 2009), 399.
3. https://www.sportskeeda.com/running/winning-olympics-barefoot-setting-records-abebe-bikilia-ethiopian-running-icon

Day One

Keep Looking to Jesus

> Therefore, since we are surrounded by so great a cloud of witnesses, let us also lay aside every weight, and sin which clings so closely, and let us run with endurance the race that is set before us, looking to Jesus, the founder and perfecter of our faith, who for the joy that was set before him endured the cross, despising the shame, and is seated at the right hand of the throne of God. Consider him who endured from sinners such hostility against himself, so that you may not grow weary or fainthearted. In your struggle against sin you have not yet resisted to the point of shedding your blood. (Hebrews 12:1–4)

Ponder Anew

Parenting is a marathon. Like a marathon, the parenting race is easier at the start, but the second half of the course gets more difficult. You give your life to rearing children through their younger years, feeding them, changing them, and sacrificing your good for theirs. Things seem to be going okay through the grade school years, but then you hit the teen years and start to feel like you are running up a steep hill, struggling to finish the race. Perhaps one of your children begins to rebel against you. Or your child deceives you, refuses to obey, or turns from your counsel to follow the foolish pleasures of the world. How do you keep running when the road gets difficult?

Nothing can keep you running through the difficulties of the parenting race like keeping your mind on Jesus. Lay aside your discouragements, your feelings of failure, your exasperation with knowing what to do, and keep Jesus in view. Consider all that Jesus went through on your behalf and be inspired to run. Jesus was rejected by his own people, deceived and betrayed by a close friend, deserted by his closest followers, falsely accused, beaten, mocked, and put to death on a cross. There, God the Father turned his face away and poured out the wrath we deserved upon Jesus. He did all this for you and, as a result of enduring earthly suffering and temptation, he is able to understand the difficulties we face and provide the encouragement and help we need to endure.

Jesus can relate to our suffering and all our parenting struggles. After all, the twelve disciples often acted like children. After three years of training, when he was most in need of their support, they all deserted him. When we feel like giving up, we should remember Christ, who cried out, "Take this cup from me" (Luke 22:42 NIV). When we suffer for the sake of the gospel—and that is what we are doing when we refuse to give up in our parenting trials—we should identify with Jesus in his suffering. The apostle Paul found comfort in counting it a privilege to suffer in the work of the gospel. He wrote:

> . . . that I may know him and the power of his resurrection, and may share his sufferings, becoming like him in his death, that by any means possible I may attain the resurrection from the dead. Not that I have already obtained this or am already perfect, but I press on to make it my own, because Christ Jesus has made me his own. Brothers, I do not consider that I have made it my own. But one thing I do: forgetting what lies behind and straining forward to what lies ahead, I press on toward the goal for the prize of the upward call of God in Christ Jesus. (Philippians 3:10–14)

Paul knew that when we suffer, we better appreciate Christ's sufferings for us. The anguish we feel when our children rebel against us is not unlike the anguish God felt at our own rebellion. So as we run our parenting race, we do not give up. We look to Christ, grateful for his salvation and the grace he demonstrated toward us. If he could save us, then he can save our children.

So keep running your parenting marathon and don't give up. Keep running, one step in front of the other, one day at a time. Keep Jesus in mind, keep the finish line in sight, and catch a second wind to keep on running.

Bring It Home

- Read Philippians 3:7–15. How is the way Paul interprets his suffering similar to what the writer of Hebrews 12:1–2 is encouraging us to do?
- How can remembering all that Jesus suffered help you endure your parenting trials?

Day Two

God Uses Parenting Trials to Refine Us

And have you forgotten the exhortation that addresses you as sons? "My son, do not regard lightly the discipline of the Lord, nor be weary when reproved by him. For the Lord disciplines the one he loves, and chastises every son whom he receives."

It is for discipline that you have to endure. God is treating you as sons. For what son is there whom his father does not discipline? If you are left without discipline, in which all have participated, then you are illegitimate children and not sons. (Hebrews 12:5–8)

Ponder Anew

Did you ever consider that the parenting trial you are going through is designed by God to help you grow? Could it be that the reason God has not brought resolution to your parenting challenge is because he is not yet finished working in your heart? So often, it is through the trials of parenting that God makes us more like his Son Jesus. We learn how to trust God. Our idols are exposed when they fail us. We learn to love as Christ loved as we love our children who treat us poorly. Through trials, we draw near to Christ and come to appreciate him as our Savior.

Think about it. If every parenting technique you used produced amazing results, imagine how self-righteous you would be. If all our children always got along, did their own devotions, served around the house, spoke respectfully, did their homework, confessed their sin when they lost their temper, and honored the other adults they met, we would assume it was because we did such a great job parenting. Now, it is not unusual for a family to have a single child that fits that mold, but if all of our children were so well-adjusted, we would be sorely tempted to take credit for that accomplishment.

The most effective and encouraging parenting seminars are those taught by men and women who have endured their own parenting struggles. They know that parenting techniques are helpful, but they cannot save or transform our children. Few things are more discouraging to a parent with a rebellious son or daughter than listening to a speaker with obedient, perfect children, who points to a long list of techniques as the way to ensure that your children do as well as his. Such advice misses the key point that God is not just after our children; he often allows parenting trials because he is also working in us.

Your difficulties in parenting may have more to do with what God is doing in your life and your family than the success or failure of your parenting techniques. Your struggles are a part of his plan. God is at work in our lives through those difficulties; he humbles us through the day-to-day trials of life. He does this out of love for us.

So if you are in the midst of a challenging trial, drop to your knees, acknowledge your inability to finish the task without him, and embrace the trial as discipline. Ask God to finish the work of transforming your heart quickly, so that you might learn all that he intends you to learn. Then pray that he will do the work in your children's hearts that only he can do.

Bring It Home

- How is God refining you in your parenting trials?
- The next time you are in a small group Bible study, ask the folks in your group this question: "Which of you rebelled against your parents before God saved you?" Then ask, "How did God work all that together for good?" The Enemy wants us to believe that we are the only family whose kids are struggling. The reality is that all around you are people God saved from foolish rebellion and sin in their teen years.

Day Three

God Disciplines Our Children Too

Besides this, we have had earthly fathers who disciplined us and we respected them. Shall we not much more be subject to the Father of spirits and live? For they disciplined us for a short time as it seemed best to them, but he disciplines us for our good, that we may share his holiness. For the moment all discipline seems painful rather than pleasant, but later it yields the peaceful fruit of righteousness to those who have been trained by it.

Therefore lift your drooping hands and strengthen your weak knees, and make straight paths for your feet, so that what is lame may not be put out of joint but rather be healed. (Hebrews 12:9–13)

Ponder Anew

Today's passage continues the discipline theme. We should not be surprised that God uses our parenting trials to discipline us. Just like an earthly father disciplines his children, so God disciplines us. That doesn't mean he is punishing us, for Jesus bore the wrath for all our sin upon the cross. God's discipline toward his children is not for retribution but for instruction, for our good. It is the pruning of the vine to produce the greater harvest. Nothing drives us to a greater dependence on God than a custom-designed trial meant to rid us of our self-confidence and self-righteousness.

Knowing that our parenting challenges are designed by God for our good can encourage us to press on in faith. Our trials are not random, they are designed by God to help us grow. Everything is directed by him. So, lift your drooping hands, strengthen your weak knees, and trust God for grace for another day.

There is another encouraging truth hidden in this passage. It comes in God's description of parenting. The writer says, "For they [our earthly fathers] disciplined us for a short time as it seemed best to them, but he [God] disciplines us for our good." Notice that we as parents only discipline for a "short time," but God's discipline continues into adulthood. So as our children grow, God takes over their discipline. We see this in the trials he brings to them, much like the trials he brings to us.

This shows up practically as well. Parental discipline is most effective with younger children, but somewhere in the teen years, our ability to discipline our older children wanes and becomes ineffective. We can tell a toddler "no" and then, if he doesn't obey, we can move him to obedience by our superior strength and size. If your three-year-old daughter refuses to put down the steak knife, you can physically remove it from her. But toddler tactics don't work very well for teens. Just try giving a rebellious teen an ultimatum—they rarely work and often make things worse.

So, rather than become frustrated at your inability to shape your teen's behavior by disciplining him into compliance, remember that God is after the heart of your teen. He is taking back the discipline he once delegated to you. Just as God custom-designs trials to rid us of our idols, he does the same for our teenage sons and daughters.

If your teen doesn't listen to you (which is something you can't force him to do), you don't need to call out the National Guard. Remind her that God is a loving Father who will discipline her because he loves her. Then watch God work. He can ensure that a son is caught in his sin and use that failure and its consequences to bring an end to his foolishness. He can bring your daughter to the end of her pride and cause her to bow her knee to Christ. Knowing that God is at work, partnering with us in the discipline of our older children, can release us from a sense that it all rests on our shoulders.

Bring It Home

- Are there any areas in which you are trying to discipline your teens like toddlers? If so, what struggles might the Lord want you to release back to him?
- Where have you seen God at work, disciplining your older children through the trials of life? Look for an

opportunity to share with your kids the ways you see God disciplining you as your loving Father. Let them know that as they get older, God in his kindness will discipline them too, for he chastises "every son whom he receives" (Hebrews 12:6).

Real Life

Going through the teenage rebellion of our oldest son, Nathan, brought Lois and me to our knees in prayer. Looking back, it is easy to see how God designed the trial of our son's rebellion to discipline us and to teach us to trust more in God than in our own strength. I'm thankful that God surrounded us with wise counselors who helped us recognize the Lord's work through what felt like a marathon. They reminded us that God was after our hearts as much as our son's. At times, it felt as though it would never end, but God was wonderfully merciful. In his perfect time, he reached down and rescued our son.

Since then, God has used our story and Nathan's testimony to encourage hundreds of parents. Having shared some of the trials we faced during Nathan's rebellion, I wanted to give Nathan the opportunity to share the testimony of his rescue, which he was eager to do. Here is Nathan's story as he tells it:

> I woke up, threw on a T-shirt and a fresh pair of jeans. It was the morning after Thanksgiving, and I knew it was going to be a fantastic day. I jumped into my car, sped down the road, and quickly arrived at a local shopping center, the usual meeting place for me and my buddies. As a young teen, I had built a reputation for questionable behavior and always needed a legitimate reason for my parents to let me go out with my friends. Today was perfect because I had a good excuse to get out of the house—Black

Friday shopping. I was filled with excitement and felt like I could conquer the world.

My friends and I piled into one vehicle and headed to the mall. After a long day of shopping and fun, we drove to the lot where we'd all parked. Once we were back at our cars, a friend pulled out a pipe of marijuana to smoke, which, unbeknownst to my parents, was something I had done with my friends before.

But this day was different. Not long after we parked, we heard sirens. I turned toward the sound and, to my dismay, saw the terrifying gleam of red and blue lights right behind our car.

Looking back, I believe that God sent that police officer. My parents had warned me. They were praying I would get caught every time I strayed. Even though I wasn't ready to live for Christ and change my ways, God allowed me to feel the weight of my sin that day. Eventually, I realized my desperate need for a Savior.

It didn't take long for the police to discover what we were doing. Within minutes, all three of us were handcuffed, placed in different cop cars, and driven to the police station down the road. My heart was racing. All I could think about was my family. How I let them down. How they would never trust or forgive me again.

Throughout my teen years, I caused trouble for my parents. I purchased a cell phone behind their back that I had delivered to a post office box I rented to keep my parents from seeing what I got in the mail. I frequently snuck out of the house late at night and began dating a girl from work without telling them what was going on. The older I got, the more opportunities I found to disobey their rules. My parents would respond in the usual way. Dad would limit my freedom, trying to prevent me from making more bad choices. He would pray for me and read the Bible with me. Dad spent countless hours meeting with me, pointing me to Jesus and trying to understand what was going on in my life. Still, I would find ways to hide what I was doing and at times I would secretly mock his attempts to control my behavior.

As I sat in the holding cell waiting for Dad to pick me up, I expected that this time I'd get an angry response. He would most certainly ground me for months, possibly even the rest of my life. At the very least, I knew that I was going to get my phone and car taken away.

Once my dad arrived, the police released me. When we got in the car, he turned to me, looked me straight in the eye, and said "I love you, son. We all make mistakes, and I believe that God had you get caught today because he has a bigger plan for you in your life." He said, "This isn't the end of the road. It's the beginning."

I wish I could say that this gracious response made me immediately change my ways. It didn't. I needed God to do that. I continued to get in trouble and lie to my family. Mom and Dad kept responding with grace and love that I certainly did not deserve. When parents respond with love (instead of anger) toward their wayward son or daughter; it demonstrates the grace of God, who does not treat us as our sins deserve. Trust me, flipping out on your kids, though they may deserve it, doesn't help them draw near to God. But love, demonstrated through kindness, breaks down the emotional barriers teens build to shut out parental advice and direction. The love of Jesus portrayed through a gracious, forgiving response can be used by God to soften their hardened hearts and open their ears to hear God's voice.

Although I believed in God and considered myself a Christian, I lived for myself. My decisions revolved around doing what I thought would make me happy. As I tried to negotiate my parents' rules, my friends from church would often make jokes about how strict our parents were, and how boring it would be to follow everything the Bible taught. As a result, I couldn't see how living for God would be any fun because much of my joy came from worldly pleasures.

Still, my selfishness and lust for sin were taking a toll on my life and my relationships, especially with my girlfriend, Lauren. She loved me, but my sneaking around, lying, and getting into trouble wasn't exactly great leadership, and was hurting our relationship. Thankfully, God continued to allow me to get caught again and again. Finally, a more serious run-in with the law resulted in the suspension of my junior driver's license. I was stopped in my tracks—literally! God used that event and its consequences to show me how careless, reckless, and immature I had been. I knew that I needed to change, but I was afraid.

I went to my parents, asking for help and forgiveness. Mom and Dad, as they had been in every other instance, forgave me with open arms and an open heart and pointed me to God. I knew that the pleasure I was chasing wasn't going to fulfill me. By the grace of God, I gave up fighting on my own and put my trust in Jesus to help me defeat my sin. I had a sense of peace and the overwhelming feeling that the Holy Spirit was with me now and forever. In the past, I had always felt that I was living my life "on the fence," but now I could confidently say which side of the fence I was on. I was filled with hope that God had a plan to use my life to bring him glory. Those years were not wasted. God had used them to show me how much I needed his grace in my life.

Dad set aside specific times to meet with me on a more regular basis, and he pointed me toward Jesus by the use of his Word. As the father from the parable in Luke 15 welcomed back the prodigal son, so my dad welcomed me back. It took some time, but I was slowly able to mend the relationships I had broken in my years of sin and selfishness. Slowly, my family began to trust me again. My friends looked up to me and respected me. And that girlfriend, Lauren, became my wife in the fall of 2015.

Your children will disobey you, and some will test you to your core. But before you respond in anger, take a step back and breathe deeply. Pray for grace, help, and guidance in disciplining your son or daughter. The gracious responses my parents demonstrated toward me opened my eyes to God's love and mercy. God can help your kids realize that same truth.

CHAPTER 18

Jesus Is Praying for You

John 17:1–26

Introduction to the Week

In 2002, our church began a ministry we named Covenant Mercies[1] as a practical way to fulfill the call of James 1:27 to care for widows and orphans. Covenant Mercies soon launched an orphan sponsorship program to help fatherless children in the rural African town of Nagongera, Uganda. The ministry now cares for more than a thousand children in Zambia, Ethiopia, and Uganda. Through a monthly or annual gift, a sponsor can provide a child with an education, clothing, nutritional support, healthcare, and, most importantly, point them to Christ through the Christian witness of local workers.

A few years ago, a teenage girl named Mesay, one of the sponsored children in Ethiopia, got into another argument with her mom. The teen left home and began living with a few of her friends in the streets of Addis Ababa. Unaware of the trouble but clearly led by the Spirit of God, Mesay's sponsor called Covenant Mercies to see if there were any ways that their family could intercede for Mesay. The Covenant Mercies staff updated the sponsors so they could pray for the girl, who was

---

1. Anyone interested in sponsoring a fatherless child through Covenant Mercies can do so through its website: covenantmercies.org/orphan-sponsorship.

scheduled to meet with Hilina, the program director in Addis. The sponsors began to intercede for Mesay and the meeting.

Past meetings with Hilina had not gone well, and Mesay came prepared to tell her that she was going to drop out of the sponsorship program to live permanently on the streets with her friends. After a rough start to the meeting, Hilina decided to pray with Mesay. From that point on, everything changed. God miraculously softened Mesay's heart and she agreed to return home. Subsequent conversations with Hilina led to her salvation and active participation in their local church.

Neither Mesay nor her mother knew that at their time of deepest struggle, a family thousands of miles away was fervently interceding for her. But they, along with Hilina, didn't pray alone. Their prayers were added to that of another intercessor, Jesus Christ, who appealed to God the Father for Mesay's life.

When we are in the depths of our struggles with our children, we can be certain that Jesus is interceding on our behalf. He is the one who can soften the hardest heart and marshal all manner of resources to help us reach our children in their deepest distress.

Day One

For Those You Have Given Me

> When Jesus had spoken these words, he lifted up his eyes to heaven, and said, "Father, the hour has come; glorify your Son that the Son may glorify you, since you have given him authority over all flesh, to give eternal life to all whom you have given him. And this is eternal life, that they know you, the only true God, and Jesus Christ whom you have sent.

I glorified you on earth, having accomplished the work that you gave me to do. And now, Father, glorify me in your own presence with the glory that I had with you before the world existed.

"I have manifested your name to the people whom you gave me out of the world. Yours they were, and you gave them to me, and they have kept your word. Now they know that everything that you have given me is from you. For I have given them the words that you gave me, and they have received them and have come to know in truth that I came from you; and they have believed that you sent me. I am praying for them. I am not praying for the world but for those whom you have given me, for they are yours. All mine are yours, and yours are mine, and I am glorified in them. And I am no longer in the world, but they are in the world, and I am coming to you. Holy Father, keep them in your name, which you have given me, that they may be one, even as we are one." (John 17:1–18)

Ponder Anew

John 17 is known as the High Priestly Prayer, for in these verses we have the opportunity to study the words Jesus prayed on our behalf to the Father. The writer of Hebrews calls Jesus our Great High Priest and we read in Hebrews 7:25 that Jesus "always lives to make intercession" for those "who draw near to God through him." Paul writes to the Romans, "Who is to condemn? Christ Jesus is the one who died—more than that, who was raised—who is at the right hand of God, who indeed is interceding for us" (Romans 8:34).

We can divide the High Priestly Prayer into three sections. First, Jesus prays for the glorification of the Father and the Son.

Then he prays for the disciples and, finally, Jesus expands his appeal to include all those who will believe in him through the Word of God. The fact that his prayer extends beyond the disciples and is intended for all believers affects the way we understand the entire prayer.

When Jesus prays, "I am praying for them"—for God the Father to keep them in his name—he is praying for all those the Father gave him to save. That includes the disciples, all of us who now believe, and all our children, who will one day bow their knee. Jesus is so certain of this accomplished work that he speaks as though the work were already complete when he says, "having accomplished the work that you gave me to do." Jesus is not only certain that he will glorify the Father through the cross, he is also sure that his sacrifice will result in the salvation of the disciples and "those whom you have given me," all those who belong to the Father.

Jesus declares that he is praying for all those the Father gave to him. He is certain that they will all keep the Father's Word and will come to know the truth that the Father sent him. Jesus prays, "Holy Father, keep them in your name, which you have given me, that they may be one, even as we are one."

As believers in Jesus Christ, we must hold onto the truth that our children are called by God to be part of his family. We have no other hope. We must believe that, by the power of God in answer to Jesus's prayers, they will come to faith. Jesus prayed the night before his crucifixion for us all, and he is still interceding before the throne of God on our behalf and our children's.

Bring It Home

- How should knowing that Jesus is at the right hand of the Father, interceding for us, affect the way we pray to Christ?

- Call out to Jesus and ask him to fulfill in your children the promises in this first portion of the High Priestly Prayer.
  1. That your children will come to know the truth of the gospel, that God the Father sent his Son to die on the cross for our sins.
  2. That they would believe in the gospel.
  3. That they would keep God's Word.
  4. That they would live in unity with other believers.

Day Two

Keep Them

"While I was with them, I kept them in your name, which you have given me. I have guarded them, and not one of them has been lost except the son of destruction, that the Scripture might be fulfilled. But now I am coming to you, and these things I speak in the world, that they may have my joy fulfilled in themselves. I have given them your word, and the world has hated them because they are not of the world, just as I am not of the world. I do not ask that you take them out of the world, but that you keep them from the evil one. They are not of the world, just as I am not of the world. Sanctify them in the truth; your word is truth. As you sent me into the world, so I have sent them into the world. And for their sake I consecrate myself, that they also may be sanctified in truth." (John 17:12–19)

Ponder Anew

Prior to praying for the disciples, Jesus taught them about his departure and the coming of the Holy Spirit. He ended that instruction with these words: "I have said these things to you, that in me you may have peace. In the world you will have tribulation. But take heart; I have overcome the world" (John 16:33). Jesus is aware that the disciples will face persecutions and attacks by the Evil One. Just moments earlier he warned Peter, "Simon, Simon, behold, Satan demanded to have you, that he might sift you like wheat, but I have prayed for you that your faith may not fail. And when you have turned again, strengthen your brothers" (Luke 22:31–32). While Jesus prayed for Peter, he did not pray against the attack, but rather that Peter's faith would not fail. Jesus knew that though the Enemy meant the trial for harm, God would use it for good.

While Jesus was with the disciples, he watched over them and guarded them so that not one of them was lost (except for Judas, whom the Scriptures describe as a unique exception). Now Jesus is aware that the cross is soon ahead of him. Shortly after his resurrection, he will return to heaven, leaving the disciples alone. So he asks the Father to watch over the disciples, to keep them from the Evil One and sanctify them. Jesus prays with a certainty that God the Father will take care of those he discipled.

Our children face the same challenges the disciples did. Praying similarly on their behalf aligns us with the heart God has for them and the prayers of Christ. Place your child's name in the blank and pray Jesus's Word over them:

"I do not ask that you take _____ out of the world, but that you keep him/her from the Evil One. Sanctify _____ in the truth; your word is truth."

We live in challenging times, and it seems that the world and the Enemy are out for our children. The easy access to inappropriate material on the web, the ease with which foolish behaviors can be shared unwisely among peers, and the increasing secularization of our culture are tempting our children away from God to pursue a lifestyle of pleasure. While it is wise to protect our children from these influences while they are young, it is impossible to guard them forever. They must face their own temptations and trials. Knowing that God can protect them and use their trials for his good and glory is a tremendous comfort. We can be advocates for our children before the Father in heaven much as Jesus lifted his disciples up before the Father.

It is important to remember that Jesus doesn't ask his Father to remove the trials of life from our children. He knows that God sanctifies them through those trials. Instead, he asks the Father to keep them while they walk through the trials designed to refine them.

Bring It Home

- What can you learn about the Father's character from the way Jesus lifted up his requests to him?
- How can the confidence Jesus had when he prayed for his disciples encourage us in our prayers for our children?

Day Three

For All Those Who Will Believe

"I do not ask for these only, but also for those who will believe in me through their word, that they may all be one, just as you, Father, are in me, and I in you, that they also may be in us, so that the world may believe that you have sent me. The glory that you have given me I have given to them, that they may be one even as we are one, I in them and you in me, that they may become perfectly one, so that the world may know that you sent me and loved them even as you loved me. Father, I desire that they also, whom you have given me, may be with me where I am, to see my glory that you have given me because you loved me before the foundation of the world. O righteous Father, even though the world does not know you, I know you, and these know that you have sent me. I made known to them your name, and I will continue to make it known, that the love with which you have loved me may be in them, and I in them." (John 17:20–26)

Ponder Anew

The words "but also for those who will believe in me" extends the prayer Jesus prayed to all believers for all time. That includes the children we are trusting God to save. We must have faith that Jesus is also praying these words for our children and that God will open our children's eyes to believe. Jesus is aware that the testimony of the disciples and their efforts to spread the gospel will not get the job done. For the whole world to believe that the Father sent Jesus, the message will need to pass onto the next generation and the one after that.

In this wonderful section of Jesus's prayer, we see the delight that exists within the unity of the Godhead and how Jesus intends this special fellowship to extend to all believers:

- That we may be one just as Jesus and the Father are one (the Father in the Son and the Son in the Father).
- That all God's people might be so unified with God that the whole world might believe in the Son.
- That Jesus might live in us as the Father lives in him.
- That the world might know that the Father loves his earthly children as much as Jesus himself, and that the same love the Father extends to Jesus might also extend to all his earthly children.
- That we might be with Jesus and see his glory.

God has existed, as Father, Son, and Spirit, in complete unity and harmony for all eternity past. It is his desire that the love and unity shared within the Godhead extend to all those he calls to be his own. That is what Jesus is praying that God the Father will do, not only for the disciples but for all "those who will believe in him."

We can never lose sight of this goal for our children, no matter how lost they appear. We must hold to the hope that they were in Christ's mind as he prayed. We can take these words back to God in prayer and pray: "O Lord, go after my children, that they may be one as you are one. Open their eyes to behold your glory and know the same love that the Father extended to Christ."

Always remember that Jesus is still praying this prayer today. He prayed two thousand years ago and he continues to intercede (Romans 8:34). We too can pray for our children in faith, with our prayers agreeing with those Jesus prayed two thousand years ago and those he is still praying in heaven.

Bring It Home

- What do we learn about God from this section of the High Priestly Prayer?
- How should the words, "but also for those who will believe in me through their word" help us apply John 17 to our own lives and the lives of our children?

Real Life

It wasn't until I sat down with Teresa that I discovered that her thirty-one-year-old son had nearly died seventy-two hours earlier from a drug overdose. He was now a few days into a thirty-day detox program at a local veterans hospital. As Teresa recounted these tragic events, she demonstrated a quiet resolve. While the trial of the past days had shaken her, Teresa's hope in

Christ came through. The grace and faith I observed could only come from trusting Jesus. Though afflicted by her son's poor choices, she wasn't bitter, for the troubles she recounted were sprinkled with sweet memories and smiles. "John is a good boy, really smart, an enterprising entrepreneur, and handsome," she said, but added, "I don't know what to do."

As I sat listening, my mind raced for words to say. *I'm not a trained drug and alcohol counselor,* I thought to myself, wondering what I should do. Though John attended our church sporadically, I'd never met him. But I knew one thing for certain; John needed Jesus. So I offered, if John was willing, to travel to the rehab center to meet with him. I asked Teresa to join me and introduce us. A few days later, the three of us sat in a Dunkin Donuts a few miles from the rehab center, where John shared his story.

He confessed that his overdose wasn't accidental; John had wanted to end his life. He explained that he had taken enough drugs to kill an elephant and shouldn't be sitting with me. In fact, he said the overdose *did* kill him before he inexplicably was brought back to life. Then he shared the story.

The paramedic found John unconscious and gave him a shot of Narcan to counteract the opiates coursing through his system. Then at regular intervals on their twenty-minute trip to the hospital, he gave John two additional doses with no response. The paramedic later told John, "I was bringing in a dead body." Then, for no explainable reason, out of sync with his protocol, the paramedic gave John's lifeless body a fourth shot. Instantly, John sprang to life; his heart was beating again. He gasped for air and began breathing. Moments later, as the ambulance pulled up to the emergency entrance, the paramedic gave John this parting advice. "I never give four shots of Narcan to anyone. I'm not even sure why I did it. All I've got to say is, you better figure out why you are alive."

Afraid that the police would send him to jail, John refused treatment at the hospital, borrowed a phone, called his mom and walked away. His dad picked him up and drove him to the veterans hospital where he enrolled in a treatment program.

John finished with this incredible part of the story. On his way to his first day's therapy, walking with another patient, John told the man he knew one thing: "I need a Bible." The next instant, as he glanced ahead, he noticed something stuck in the railing in front of them. John went over and pulled out a Bible wedged between the steel bars. When he opened the front cover, there was an inscription which said, "For a veteran in need."

John looked up from his coffee with a blank, hopeless expression. He said, "I don't know what to do." I didn't have all the answers, but I knew I could give John the answer to the question the paramedic posed. I knew why John was alive. There was only one logical explanation: Jesus intended to save him. You didn't need to be Sherlock Holmes to put the pieces of the story together. Jesus was after John.

After sharing the gospel with John, he quickly admitted his need and asked God to save him. Later that night, he called his cousin Destin, whose life he'd seen God transform. They grew up together, got into trouble together, and now John wanted his advice. He asked, "How do I follow God?" and "How can I be free? I feel so unqualified. I've sinned way too much to go to heaven." Destin shared the gospel, and John again called out to God. Destin remembered his prayer. "God," John said, "I believe in you. Please forgive me for my sin; I know it's a lot. Help me to get free and follow you. Thank you, Jesus, for dying on the cross for me." That night John put his head on the pillow as a child of the King. The Holy Spirit regenerated John's heart and brought him into God's family. He began reading his Bible and came back to church.

Tragically, John's life didn't last long. His roommate at the rehab found him unresponsive one morning, just as he finished his thirty days and was entering a new phase of treatment. God saved him, then called him home.

Teresa asked Destin to share at the funeral. It wasn't until listening to his eulogy that I learned that my son-in-law had been reaching out to John all along. Destin shared the details of the prayer John prayed the night after my first visit. Afterwards, Destin and John started reading the Gospel of John. They texted often, and John called Destin to talk about all that he was learning. John shared his desire to follow Jesus and get baptized. Destin closed his funeral message with these words:

> In short, the amazing story of John being saved is that God patiently kept him alive long enough to show him the beauty of our crucified Savior, Jesus Christ. John turned away from his sins and believed in him, and has eternal life! What a merciful God! God did the same for our cousin Derrick, who went home to be with the Lord about this time last year. God also did the same for me, and I am convinced that the reason God left me on this earth a little longer is to tell all of you this good news, that you can be saved too! John's story is still being written, and I believe that a chapter is being written right now as I speak. Perhaps God took John now so that we could all hear this news today and believe it and be together forever with Jesus.

God was writing another chapter. John's sister, Jess, and his girlfriend, Lauren, were crushed by the grief of his passing, but God had a plan to save them both. In God's providence, Lauren lived directly across the street from Emma and Destin. They reached out to her and invited her to Bridge, our church evangelistic Bible study. Jess joined her, as they both had planned to go with John to Bridge. They thought it would be a great way to honor him now that he was gone. God used the course to draw them to Christ, and both women said that they would never have come to Christ if not for what happened to John. They were baptized two Sundays apart in front of our whole church.

Lauren shared, "Over the last few weeks, I've come to trust and believe wholeheartedly that I've been saved. I have repented of my sins and believed in Jesus Christ alone for salvation. I still struggle with certain things, like my sadness and suffering through John's death, and there is more to my story. But with the blessing of God's grace and mercy, I know he will see me through and love me when I can't love myself. I am a Christian, and I want to serve God and be able to help others find God's love as time moves forward."

When all hell and evil were bent on stealing one of God's children, God refused and pulled John from the clutches of death to save him. Then he used those events to save at least two of those gathered for the memorial service, and likely more. Jesus said in his prayer, "I have guarded them, and not one of them has been lost" (John 17:12). That was true of his disciples, and it is true of John, his sister, and his girlfriend, and all "those who will believe" (John 17:20).

CHAPTER 19

Don't Be Shaken

Psalm 16

Introduction to the Week

A few years ago, I experienced my first earthquake. I could feel the undulating ripples of the ground rolling like a gentle sea. Yet these subtle rolls jarred the walls of our church office and shook the pictures on the walls. Within a few minutes, the motion stopped. The minor quake did not damage our two-story building, but I was amazed at how much vibration the tremor caused. It was easy to see how a more violent earthquake could destroy a building. The taller the building, the more susceptible it is to the movement caused by an earthquake. Engineers have come up with some remarkable devices to protect larger structures from collapsing.

Perhaps the most interesting of these devices is the giant ball that builders suspended in the Taipei 101, located in Taipei, Taiwan. A giant steel ball, eighteen feet in diameter, is suspended by eight cables between floors 87 and 92 in this 101-story building. It weighs 728 tons (nearly a million and a half pounds) and can sway five feet in any direction. If the skyscraper swings left, the ball pulls right in the opposite direction, like your head does when it hits the headrest of an airplane seat at takeoff. The resulting force of this mega-ball pulls the skyscraper in the opposite direction from the movement caused by the quake, thus stabilizing the building. If you are ever in Taipei, you can view the large tuned mass damper (which is what the device is called), from an observation deck. There you can see it sway against the wind on a blustery day or in an earthquake, as guests experienced on May 12, 2008.

The Bible uses the analogy of shaking to describe the trials we experience in life. We, like Taipei 101, have a tuned mass damper to help us during life's tremors. We turn to the Scriptures, which point us to God, who holds us fast. Psalm 16, our focus this week, is one of the Bible passages the Spirit of God uses to anchor us during times of shaking.

Day One

Preserve Me, O God

> Preserve me, O God, for in you I take refuge. I say to the LORD, "You are my Lord; I have no good apart from you."
>
> As for the saints in the land, they are the excellent ones, in whom is all my delight.
>
> The sorrows of those who run after another god shall multiply; their drink offerings of blood I will not pour out or take their names on my lips. (Psalm 16:1–4)

Ponder Anew

David opens his prayer with these words, "Preserve me, O God, for in you I take refuge." We know that there were many times in his life when David had no place to turn but God. His trials were so fierce that only in God could he find rest.

His simple prayer carries a deeper truth, for the New Testament writers who quote David indicate that his words are prophetic. (We'll examine those references in more detail later this week.) As David calls out amid his own trial, he is pointing toward Christ, whose trials also pressed him to cry out for help. David foreshadows the Savior; his faith in trial and trust in God is a picture of Christ and a lesson for us. As David found his refuge in God, so Jesus found his hope in his gracious Father, and so too must we look to God for our deliverance and comfort.

David moves on from his introductory prayer to contrast the saints, whose seeking after God comforts us in trials, with the idolaters who reject him and pull our gaze away from God. There is a great comfort to be found in sharing your troubles with other believers. They become the hands and feet of Christ to us, sharing with us the wisdom of his Word. They encourage us with the encouragement that they have themselves received from Christ (2 Corinthians 1:4), and they can keep our focus upon Jesus when we waver in our faith.

But there is also a sobering message to be found in the comparison: we should not find ourselves numbered with those who run after other gods. When we've cried out to God but do not hear an answer, or when we've asked God to deliver us but no deliverance comes, the Enemy is ever ready to throw his fiery darts at us, to tempt us to reject the Lord.

We must, like David, remain resolute in finding our hope and help in God alone. He is our refuge; like David, we must declare our trust in him and steer our lives toward the safe harbor of Christ. When our faith is weak, it helps to speak out the very things we are struggling to believe and ask God for help. We must declare that our belief and hope rest in Christ alone.

Bring It Home

- Where do you battle for faith? Where are you most tempted to give up?
- How can speaking out about what we struggle to believe help us stand strong?

Day Two

I Shall Not Be Shaken

> The LORD is my chosen portion and my cup; you hold my lot. The lines have fallen for me in pleasant places; indeed, I have a beautiful inheritance.
>
> I bless the LORD who gives me counsel; in the night also my heart instructs me. I have set the LORD always before me; because he is at my right hand, I shall not be shaken. (Psalm 16:5–8)

Ponder Anew

The shaking of the world by God described in Scripture refers to his judgment. The writer of Hebrews is speaking of this judgment when he declares:

> At that time his voice shook the earth, but now he has promised, "Yet once more I will shake not only the earth but also the heavens." This phrase, "Yet once more," indicates the removal of things that are shaken—that is, things that have been made—in order that the things that cannot be shaken may remain. Therefore let us be grateful for receiving a kingdom that cannot be shaken, and thus let us offer

to God acceptable worship, with reverence and awe, for our God is a consuming fire. (Hebrews 12:26–29)

As Christians, we are spared God's final judgment because Jesus took the punishment for our sin. So how are we to understand the shaking we all endure as believers? As we have already seen, our trials are designed to purify us to make us more like Jesus. For us, the shaking trials of God are meant to dislodge and jettison everything that can be shaken—the unbelief and idolatry of remaining sin. But who we are in Christ will not be shaken away. Like a throw rug shaken outdoors to remove dust and dirt, God shakes us to purify us for his service. When we are shaken by trials, our sin is shaken away, but we remain steadfast in Christ.

David knows these truths. He has come to trust the Lord amid his trials, and because God is his chosen portion, he knows he "shall not be shaken." He knows that God is in control of his life; God holds his lot. Knowing he's been given a "beautiful inheritance" changes David's perspective on life. Though Saul tried to kill him, though David fell in adultery, though two of his sons rebelled and sought to take his throne, David declares, "The lines have fallen for me in pleasant places."

How is this outlook possible? David finds his rest and fulfillment in knowing God, his "chosen portion." David's confidence comes not from how well he has done in life, but from knowing that he is aligned with God and therefore need not fear the ultimate shaking of God's judgment. He knows that because he stands with God, he will not be shaken.

David's rest in God does not depend on the circumstances of his life; it depends on David's confidence that God is his portion and his cup—his food and drink, which feeds him during life's storms.

God uses parenting trials to shake us so that what can be shaken will fall away and what cannot be shaken will remain. Sometimes he will allow our worst fears for our children to materialize—a pregnant daughter, a tragic accident, a serious illness, or a revelation of hidden sin to show us that he is bigger than those trials. For some of us, it takes walking on the waves of the storm to experience our lack of faith as we sink, and his salvation when we cry, like Peter, "Lord, save me" (Matthew 14:30).

Truth from passages like Psalm 16 provides the food and drink we need to find grace for another day. Our hope is in an eternal kingdom that cannot be shaken and in knowing that God holds the trials of our lives in check. Remembering these truths helps us to see that despite the difficulties we face, our lines have fallen in pleasant places. The most difficult of our parenting trials are temporary, not eternal, and that makes all the difference. We can endure the shaking because we, in Christ, cannot be shaken.

Bring It Home

- What do you think God is trying to shake away through the trials he designed for you?
- How can seeing our lives through the lens of an eternal kingdom help us gain perspective on our trials?
- We know from Scripture that David endured great trials throughout his life. What can we learn from the lyrics he wrote in Psalm 16?

Day Three

He Will Not Abandon You

> Therefore my heart is glad, and my whole being rejoices; my flesh also dwells secure. For you will not abandon my soul to Sheol, or let your holy one see corruption.
>
> You make known to me the path of life; in your presence there is fullness of joy; at your right hand are pleasures forevermore. (Psalm 16:9–11)

Ponder Anew

David's confidence that God would hold him fast through his trials came from his belief in God's unshakable plan. God told him through the prophet Nathan that God would establish his house and his kingdom forever (2 Samuel 7:16). David firmly believed that God would not abandon him to the grave. As David declared his faith through Psalm 16, the Spirit of God inspired his words to point forward to his deliverance— through the resurrection of Jesus. Because the grave could not hold Jesus and he rose again, David was saved. We have the very same hope.

Peter, inspired by the Holy Spirit, told the crowd gathered at Pentecost that these words of Psalm 16 foretold Christ's resurrection. Peter said:

> ". . . this Jesus, delivered up according to the definite plan and foreknowledge of God, you crucified and killed by the hands of lawless men. God raised him up, loosing the pangs of death, because it was not possible for him to be held by it. For David

says concerning him, 'I saw the Lord always before me, for he is at my right hand that I may not be shaken; therefore my heart was glad, and my tongue rejoiced; my flesh also will dwell in hope. For you will not abandon my soul to Hades, or let your Holy One see corruption. You have made known to me the paths of life; you will make me full of gladness with your presence.'" (Acts 2:23–28)

Paul likewise applies David's words to Christ's resurrection (Acts 13:35–37). While David saw a shadow of God's plan at best, he still believed. He trusted God over his circumstances, which helps us understand David's opening words. "Preserve me, O God, for in you I take refuge. I say to the LORD, "You are my Lord; I have no good apart from you."

Like David, we cannot allow our daily challenges to rob us of our eternal hope, for it is in that hope that we find joy. Our joy, birthed in trusting God, sustains us in our trial and helps us to trust God even more, which leads to a fullness of joy that no trial can take away from us. Then we, like David, can say, "You make known to me the path of life; in your presence there is fullness of joy; at your right hand are pleasures forevermore."

Bring It Home

- How can trusting in God's promises help us grow in our joy despite our trials?
- When it comes to parenting, our confidence must be based on God, not in our own ability. Read through Psalm 16 again. Which verses reveal David placing his trust in God?

Real Life

I first met David and Grace Stanley the hard way—over the phone, as the children's pastor, calling them to apologize. That Sunday, one of my workers had told David that their son Lang was no longer welcome in the classroom. Lang had been disruptive, but we should have engaged his parents much differently. By the time I found out, David and Grace were already gone. When I spoke with him over the phone, David graciously forgave me and agreed to give our ministry a second chance at caring for his son. Then he revealed a long history of rejection from churches because of their children's special needs.

Their calling to care for children in need began two months after they were married when, due to his mother's illness, David and Grace welcomed his younger brother and sister (five and eight years old) into their home, where they remained until adulthood. After adding four natural-born children to their clan, they answered a call to serve in a pilot foster day-care program. Their experience as part-time foster parents moved them to become full-time foster parents. Shortly thereafter, they added baby Grace to the Stanley family. Baby Grace lived with them for eighteen months. When they expressed an interest in adopting Grace, they were denied because of the color of their skin. Grace was then given up for adoption to another couple, leaving the Stanleys heartbroken.

That didn't stop the agency from placing another foster child in the Stanley home. Tina was diagnosed with a condition called "failure to thrive." Tina suffered from seizures and was profoundly mentally handicapped. Part of her brain never developed. David fought vigorously as her advocate in a health care system where foster children often slipped through the cracks. The Stanleys were moved by God's charge to Israel from Leviticus 19: "When a stranger sojourns with you in your land, you shall not do him wrong. You shall treat the stranger who sojourns with you as the native among you, and you shall love him as yourself, for you were strangers in the land of Egypt: I am the LORD your God" (Leviticus 19:33–34).

Even with the best of care, Tina never went beyond the developmental level of a six-month-old. She became their first adopted daughter and thrived in the love-saturated Stanley home until the Lord took her home to glory at age fifteen. When I asked David and Grace how they have remained unshaken through the devastating losses and challenges in caring for children like Tina, David said, "It is God's sovereignty that holds me. I believe he is in control of every detail of the universe and every detail of my life. 'And we know that for those who love God all things work together for good' (Romans 8:28). I may not always know how the circumstances of life will unfold, but I know they are there for my good. We are clay in the potter's hands, or like the dough my wife Grace pounds as she kneads it on the board. He is making us useful. God has a purpose. I might not see it now, but one day he will make it known. God gave us these children; how could we not take them in?"

Three years after taking in Tina, the Stanleys were asked to take in Niki, an infant with a tracheotomy. "Since Tina was easy," David shared, "we figured we could handle another child. After all, we thought, how hard could it be to care for a child with a trach?"

They soon found that it was hard, very hard. The day they received Niki, the medical staff told the Stanleys that she would likely have the trach in for five to seven years and said it was unlikely that she would ever be capable of much physical activity. "Don't be surprised if she doesn't make it through the night," one doctor warned. Niki made it through the night in spite of her trach, feeding tube, oxygen feed, and heart monitor.

Many meds were dispensed day and night and Niki's trach tube required suctioning every two hours around the clock.

Caring for her was a full-time endeavor. Day by day the Stanleys trusted God to supply the needed grace as their family poured love and care upon frail Niki. In God's kindness, the trach came out much sooner, at her second birthday. Defying the predictions of the doctors, Niki thrived on the love of the Stanley home. By the time she reached high school, she ran track and played soccer. As their second officially adopted daughter, Niki still lives with David and Grace today.

The story goes on with child after child, some staying years, others passing through within months. The Stanleys were chosen to take in a little boy named Sam, one of the first infants diagnosed with pediatric AIDS. (That was back in the early nineties when nobody understood AIDS.) The disease took its toll and Sam died just before his third birthday. Reflecting back on their calling and its challenges, David said, "God places your child into your home for a reason. They are a gift, but they are not really yours; they belong to God. You may not understand all the whys behind their challenges, but it is an opportunity to fully rely on God. When difficulties confronted us, Grace and I didn't have to stop and wonder what to do—you just prayed, did your part, and waited on God." He added, "I still grieve the loss of the children who passed into glory but am comforted by the love of God. I know where they are. I know I will see them again. I'm at peace with that. I just keep coming back to the truth that God's in control. He is doing all things well, and therefore I'm not shaken—I'm not."

Grace became pregnant and gave birth to Kay, who grew up to love and care for her multifaceted family as an extra set of hands God designed to help David and Grace. Lang joined the Stanleys as a malnourished six-month-old when Kay was only three. He was subsequently diagnosed with autism and is the child who led to the phone call that introduced me to Grace and David. One evening Lang announced to Grace,

"If you love me, you'll adopt me. You say you love me; do you?" Eight years into his foster care, David and Grace adopted Lang.

Becky and Ginny, twin sisters, were the last two children to join the Stanley clan. Becky was diagnosed with cerebral palsy, and her sister was born seriously frail, needing acute care. Both survived against the odds and were later adopted by the Stanleys. Today, when Becky rides into the church in her motorized wheelchair, she is eager to point out how she and her dad are wearing matching colors. David smiles one of those smiles that lights up a whole room. He and Grace have given up a lot in this life, but have gained so much love. And if we could see the treasure they are storing up in glory—well, let's just say that God will not be outdone.

In addition to his two siblings and their five natural-born children, David and Grace have cared for twenty-five foster children, five of whom they've adopted. Their lives shine as our church looks for the grace we need to follow their example. Their testimony in caring for multiple special-needs children encourages those who are trying to fight for faith to care for one.

David shared, "You know, it says in Hebrews 13 that when you welcome strangers into your home, you never know when you might be entertaining angels. Could the kids we've welcomed into our home be angels, with us unaware? I don't know that they are angels, but our little angels taught us and were sent by God to bless us." Grace added, "As much love as we gave them, they gave us more."

CHAPTER 20

God Planned It All to Save
Ephesians 1:1–15

Introduction to the Week

The ancient Greek mathematician Pythagoras is credited with discovering the equation that is now named after him; we call it the Pythagorean Theorem. Mathematically it looks like this: $a^2 + b^2 = c^2$ and is used by every student of Euclidean geometry. In simple terms, it helps you figure out the length of the long side of a right triangle based on the lengths of the two short sides. It works every time. Mathematical equations are wonderful because they are always true.

There are also theological equations in the Bible that are always true. For example, "God is eternal." God always was and always will be. Mathematically, you could write that out as $G\infty$. There is another theological truth that we can write in the form of an equation that blows my mind. I call it the Great Grace Equation. Here it is: God's Gifts + God's Good Works + God's Grace = Our Gain. Mathematically you could write this out as $GG+GGG+GG=OG$.

Think about it. God gives us gifts (1 Corinthians 12:1–11) that we exercise to accomplish the good works he has prepared for us to walk in (Ephesians 2:10). We are fueled by his grace and power (1 Corinthians 15:10), but in the end, he awards us for the work he accomplished through us (2 Timothy 4:7–8).

That is amazing! Did you notice that we, who end up getting credit, are not doing much in this equation? (There is only one "O" in that string of "G's"!). God sovereignly works all things according to his purpose for our good, which is designed by God to provoke our praise.

It is only by his gifts, plan, and grace that we can accomplish anything. Remembering that can relieve the pressure we would otherwise feel to transform the hearts of our children. Just as we relied on God to save us, we rely on him for our kids too. When life appears to spiral out of control, knowing that God remains in control, directing all things according to the counsel of his will for our good, can bring us peace in the midst of our parenting storm.

Day One

Chosen and Predestined

> Grace to you and peace from God our Father and the Lord Jesus Christ. Blessed be the God and Father of our Lord Jesus Christ, who has blessed us in Christ with every spiritual blessing in the heavenly places, even as he chose us in him before the foundation of the world, that we should be holy and blameless before him. In love he predestined us for adoption as sons through Jesus Christ, according to the purpose of his will, to the praise of his glorious grace, with which he has blessed us in the Beloved. (Ephesians 1:2–6)

Ponder Anew

After a short greeting, Paul opens his letter with a panoramic review of the grace involved in our salvation. Here are a few of the amazing statements contained in these first few verses:

- God the Father blessed us in Christ with every spiritual blessing in the heavenly places. While Paul doesn't include a list of these spiritual blessings here, it is clear that because of Jesus we have entrance into heaven all based on what Jesus did, not our efforts.
- God chose us in Christ before the foundation of the world. Here again, we have Christ to thank. God did not base his choice on our future good works. It was because he loved us that he sent his Son to take our sin to the cross, that we might be found blameless in Christ.
- God makes us holy and blameless before him. Not only did God choose us, he took responsibility for our renovation. It does not say that God chose us because we made ourselves holy and blameless, but that our holiness is a product of this process of blessing and grace.
- God adopted us as sons through Jesus Christ. Now we see a further explanation for why we are afforded all the spiritual blessings of heaven. God adopted us as his sons and daughters and welcomes us into the royal family of heaven.

How is this passage relevant to parents with struggling children? It describes all that God does in the great salvation equation. Our children are not saved by their works, nor are they saved by our efforts. Parents try to carry the responsibility for their children's salvation on their own shoulders when in fact it is all of grace from first to last. We did not save ourselves, nor can we save our children. God uses our efforts and prayers to reach our kids and weaves those works into his wonderful tapestry of grace, but even that small contribution is only possible because God first gave us the grace to do it. Here is the most comforting truth of all: the salvation and transformation of our children rests on God and his work through Christ, not us.

Once Scripture convinces us that salvation for our children is by grace alone, we must reject the accusations of the Enemy that would exclude our children from the number of the redeemed. "Your children are not good enough." "They are not chosen by God." "They are too rebellious to be saved." But these lies spring from his desperation. Remember, he is a liar.

Review the testimonies of a handful of your Christian friends and they will remind you of the saving power of God. In even the smallest sampling, we find men and women who rebelled against their parents and refused to believe, yet God was able, through trial and storm, love and grace, to bring them home into the kingdom.

We can entrust our burden for our children's salvation to God while we purpose to live for Christ. In that way our lives stand as signposts pointing them to Jesus. Where the Spirit provides us with an opportunity, we should share the gospel and plead with them to turn to Jesus. The rest is up to God.

Bring It Home

- Why is it often easier to see God's grace for ourselves and other people's children than it is for our children?
- Where can we find comfort in this passage for children who have completely turned from God?

Day Two

According to the Purpose of God

> In him we have redemption through his blood, the
> forgiveness of our trespasses, according to the riches

of his grace, which he lavished upon us, in all wisdom and insight making known to us the mystery of his will, according to his purpose, which he set forth in Christ as a plan for the fullness of time, to unite all things in him, things in heaven and things on earth.

In him we have obtained an inheritance, having been predestined according to the purpose of him who works all things according to the counsel of his will, so that we who were the first to hope in Christ might be to the praise of his glory. (Ephesians 1:7–14)

Ponder Anew

It is clear from these verses that God isn't winging it when it comes to our salvation or the salvation of our children. He has a plan and works all things according to the counsel of his will. This means that God can steer the worst of Satan's attacks to accomplish his predetermined, eternal plan. Though the crucifixion was the evil work of men, God used the cross to accomplish our salvation. Peter proclaimed this truth at Pentecost when he said, "Therefore let all Israel be assured of this: God has made this Jesus, whom you crucified, both Lord and Messiah" (Acts 2:36 NIV). While the powers of darkness thought they were winning, they were facilitating the ultimate defeat of evil.

God never authors evil, but he can steer evil to accomplish his intended purpose. We see God's ability to use evil to accomplish his plan in the way he used the conquest of the Babylonians to discipline his people. Habakkuk writes, "Look among the nations, and see; wonder and be astounded. For I am doing a work in your days that you would not believe if told. For behold, I am raising up the Chaldeans, that bitter and hasty nation, who march through the breadth of the earth, to seize dwellings not their own" (Habakkuk 1:5–6).

The story of Joseph is another classic example. His brothers sell him into slavery, Joseph is falsely accused and thrown in prison, but in the end, God uses all of that for the salvation of the very brothers who committed the original crime. Joseph said, "You intended to harm me, but God intended it for good, to accomplish what is now being done, the saving of many lives" (Genesis 50:20 NIV).

Before the foundation of the earth was laid, God set forth a plan to unite all things in and through Christ. He is determined not to lose a single one of his children. He bends all of history toward his will and purpose. No sin of man or wicked work of darkness can stand against God.

Unfortunately, things don't always go according to our plans. Every parent imagines that their children will grow up to follow the Lord at a young age and honor their father and mother. Sure, we know there will be bumps in the road, but no parent ever thinks that their cute little girl or darling boy will turn resolutely against God and refuse all appeals to live for God.

Understanding God's sovereign authority and power over all things can help us rest when life doesn't follow our plans. In those moments we learn how helpless and dependent we are, and how powerful God is. When a son or daughter's rebellion can't be checked by mom or dad, it is a comfort to know that God isn't stymied as we are. He is working all in conformity to the counsel of his will. The response for us is to join with his efforts through our prayers and place our trust in him.

Bring It Home

- Where have you seen God use evil to accomplish his good, working things to fulfill his master plan?
- Where would you like to see God work evil for good in the life of your children? Formulate these desires into a prayer and offer it up to God.

Day Three

Sealed and Guaranteed

> In him you also, when you heard the word of truth, the gospel of your salvation, and believed in him, were sealed with the promised Holy Spirit, who is the guarantee of our inheritance until we acquire possession of it, to the praise of his glory. (Ephesians 1:13–14)

Ponder Anew

How many times did you hear the gospel before you believed? For me, it was dozens of times. I knew the facts of the gospel but never understood that Jesus died for my sin personally. Then one day, as I watched a TV evangelist explain the personal implications of Christ's death, God opened my eyes to the truth and softened my heart to believe. That was when the Spirit of God came into my life.

Everyone's salvation story is different, but we have one thing in common: it was the gospel message that God used to save us. While God is the one who softens a person's heart to believe, we can join with God on this mission by sharing the gospel message with our kids and living out our relationship with God before them. In the gospel, we have the words of life that God can use at any moment to transform their lives. Some reject the gospel again and again until, at the perfect moment in the plan of God, the words suddenly spring to life in their minds and they are converted.

When God regenerates a person's heart, he seals their inheritance by taking up residence within them. Paul indicates that when the Spirit of God comes to live inside us, we have a witness to his presence in our lives. We know he is there. How else would the Spirit be our guarantee until the time when we take possession of the fullness of God's promises? God living in us begins his transforming work to make us more like Jesus. This work produces a changed life, with our cooperation, which springs from our changed desires. That is why the Bible describes our salvation as a conversion (Acts 15:3). We were living for ourselves and then, suddenly, our desires changed so that we began to live for God. People can see the change in us, and God uses this transformation to increase their desire for the same.

Our Spirit-filled life adds credibility to our gospel testimony before our children. He transforms our motives and affections and gives us a newfound love for Christ. Countless thousands of children have been led to faith by remembering the relationship their parents had with the God they rejected. They may say they reject our belief system, but our lives become the standard for their understanding of spiritual fulfillment. They may go on a quest to discover truth and explore any number of spiritual paths, but we know from Scripture that gods of wood and stone give no reply and offer no relationship.

So, don't underestimate the power of your testimony as you live out your relationship with God before your children. You don't need to be perfect, just faithful. God can reach your kids as they watch your confession and repentance, just as easily as he can through your faithful devotion. Your interaction with God's Spirit in both devotion and confession validates God's reality and creates in your kids a thirst for knowing God.

Bring It Home

- Where have you seen the Spirit of God at work in your life? Have you ever shared with your children what God is doing in your life?

- Write out your conversion story as a letter to your son or daughter. Tell them in the letter that you wanted to make sure that they had a record of what God has done in your life. Explain in the concluding paragraphs how God has changed your desires, affections, and dreams. Be sure to include the gospel, but don't use the letter to correct them. Instead, allow the Holy Spirit to use the testimony of your conversion to reach them.

Real Life

As I conclude this book, I'm looking over a beautiful lake in the wilderness of rural Maine, on a writing retreat sabbatical. Yesterday my wife and I kayaked to the far side of the lake, where a bald eagle swept across our path on a fishing run, not more than forty yards away. All around the lake, moss hangs from weathered branches of trees. The earth of the forest at the far end of the lake is so soft and loamy that I imagine that my feet are the only ones to have trod upon it for the past hundred years. But my escape into the beautiful wilderness will shortly come to an end. Soon, I'll hit the traffic of New York City on my way home. It's a trial that you know is coming, you just don't know how difficult it will be. Life is like that.

While I've written the real-life accounts at the end of each chapter to encourage parents with stories of hope and rescue, they are only snapshots into lives of real people who continue to struggle and endure. That is the nature of our lives on earth until the Lord returns or brings us home. Until then, I fully expect God's refining trials to continue, along with his sustaining grace to endure.

Several of the stories I've written about are still unfolding. We are not in heaven yet, and the Lord has not yet returned. So for me, like every believer, I know there will be additional hardships as well as added rescues. The same God who delivered us in the past will be at the rudder with those new challenges, steering a course to our ultimate safe harbor, our heavenly home in a re-created earth. Only then will every tear be wiped away and all evil, temptation, and sin be banished forever.

That is something we all must labor to remember. Too often I crave a peace-filled, trouble-free life here on earth. It's not that I don't want Christ; it's more that I can be okay enjoying my comfortable first-world life six days a week and think of Jesus on Sunday. But God is faithful to allow the troubles of this world to bring me back to a place of need. Each time his fatherly trials arrive, I learn fresh dependence upon my Rock in the storm, and he comforts me. Then as time passes, I find that the trials of life increase both my dissatisfaction with this broken world and my desire for our Lord's return.

Until he comes upon the clouds or takes me home, I try to live my days with a sense of longing. The trouble-free moments I enjoy, by the grace of God, like my time on this lake, point to heaven, but I am wise enough to know that it is not yet heaven, though my flesh wants it to be.

There are other stories I have not included in this book—ongoing tales of sorrow and heartbreak that God has yet to resolve. I know parents whose children have not yet returned home and remain prodigals. There are parents whose children claim a relationship with Christ but are living for the treasures of this world. Still other parents are estranged from their children and are fervently praying for a restored relationship. In short, this world we live in is broken. Our hope is not in this life, but in a life yet to come. If God has not yet answered your prayers, do not give up. There is no hope in giving up, but there is great hope in trusting God for the salvation of our children and the restoration of our relationship with them.

One day the traffic delays of New York City will be banished, and we'll enjoy a world of everlasting peace with Christ. In heaven, we'll have all the time we need to enjoy a lifetime of

Help your family rediscover the treasure of the gospel and the wisdom of God's Word

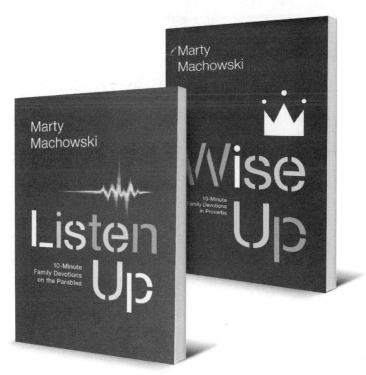

Listen Up: Ten-Minute Devotions on the Parables and
Wise Up: Ten-Minute Family Devotions in Proverbs
by Marty Machowski offer gospel truths told in simple,
easy-to-understand stories, activities, songs, and more,
helping kids identify with Jesus and grow in intimacy with God.

years living along every quiet lake. We'll take time to share the testimony of God's faithfulness with one another, and that will be a lot of stories! I look forward to meeting you to swap stories of God's deliverance and give him thanks and praise. Look me up once we're there! You'll find me fishing on a lake, climbing a mountain, or swimming on the shore of some tropical beach, enjoying the warmth of the clear, clean, sparkling surf. We'll pull up a chair, invite the Lord to join us, and speak of his faithfulness. I promise to spend days with each of you, hearing all your stories—we'll have plenty of time. While I don't yet know the details that will fill the days between now and then, I do know the outcome—Jesus will be glorified and found faithful to the last.